Climbing the Ladder of Business Intelligence

Happy About Creating Excellence through Enabled Intuition

**By James E. Cates
Sam S. Gill
Natalie Zeituny**

21265 Stevens Creek Blvd.
Suite 205
Cupertino, CA 95014

Climbing the Ladder of Business Intelligence: Happy About Creating Excellence through Enabled Intuition

First Printing: April, 2007
Paperback ISBN: 1-60005-043-3
Place of Publication: Silicon Valley, California, USA
Library of Congress Number: 2007925200

eBook ISBN: 1-60005-044-1

Trademarks

All terms mentioned in this book that are known to be trademarks or service marks have been appropriately capitalized. Happy About® cannot attest to the accuracy of this information. Use of a term in this book should not be regarded as affecting the validity of any trademark or service mark. The LOBI® trademark is owned by James E. Cates.

Warning and Disclaimer

Every effort has been made to make this book as complete and as accurate as possible, but no warranty of fitness is implied. The information provided is on an "as is" basis. The authors and the publisher shall have neither liability nor responsibility to any person or entity with respect to any loss or damages arising from the information contained in this book.

Praise for Climbing the Ladder of Business Intelligence (from the back cover)

"Cates, Gill and Zeituny have developed an easy conceptual tool "The Ladder" that captures the essence of modern business teachings. The authors have been able to invisibly integrate a vast amount of theoretical business concepts into an easy to learn framework for organizational success. The integrated case example throughout the book captures the interest of the reader as does a good novel. I would find this book a valuable addition to numerous business school courses such as Leadership, Organizational Design and Change, Decision Making, and Strategy. The book provides a clear process to improve the "intelligence quotient" of any organization and if followed, allow the organization to achieve a state of continuous organizational learning and improvement in a business environment of rapid change. This is a book that belongs on the active desk of a manager, not the bookshelf."

John A. Dopp, Director, Graduate Business Programs, Professor of Management, College of Business, San Francisco State University

Publisher

- Mitchell Levy, http://www.happyabout.info/

Cover Designer

- Cate Calson, http://www.calsongraphics.com/

Layout Designer

- Val Swisher, President, Oak Hill Corporation http://www.oakhillcorporation.com/

Copy Editor

- Valerie Hayes

Dedication

I would like to dedicate this book to my mother and father, James and Ada V. Cates, for their unconditional love, support and guidance during my formative years. The two of them created my life view which has sustained me through good times and bad. Also, I dedicate this book to my wife, Mary, for her enduring patience.

I dedicate the writings to the hundreds of employees that have given me input on the LOBI® framework over the years. It was through your requests that I knew it must be documented. Finally, I dedicate the writings to my two co-authors, Sam and Natalie, who I have become friends with during this book creation. Without their Insight and efforts, this book would never have been completed.

James E. Cates

I would like to dedicate this manuscript to Leni and James Sassower for inspiring, encouraging, and believing in me.

Sam S. Gill

I would like to dedicate the book to my mom and dad -- Lucy and Salim Zeituny for their infinite love and faith in me.

I dedicate the writings to all my friends, my extended family and to all the teachers who guided, believed and supported me along the way through personal transitions and professional aspirations.

Natalie Zeituny

A Message From Happy About®

Thank you for your purchase of this Happy About book. It is available online at http://happyabout.info/climbing-ladder.php or at other online and physical bookstores.

- Please contact us for quantity discounts at sales@happyabout.info
- If you want to be informed by e-mail of upcoming Happy About® books, please e-mail bookupdate@happyabout.info

Happy About is interested in you if you are an author who would like to submit a non-fiction book proposal or a corporation that would like to have a book written for you. Please contact us by e-mail editorial@happyabout.info or phone (1-408-257-3000).

Other Happy About books available include:

- Overcoming Inventoritis: http://happyabout.info/overcoming-inventoritis.php
- Happy About People-to-People Lending With Prosper.com: http://happyabout.info/prosper/
- Happy About Online Networking: http://happyabout.info/onlinenetworking.php
- Happy About Apartment Management: http://happyabout.info/apartment-management.php
- Confessions of a Resilient Entrepreneur: http://happyabout.info/confessions-entrepreneur.php
- Memoirs of the Money Lady: http://happyabout.info/memoirs-money-lady.php
- 30-Day Bootcamp: Your Ultimate Life Makeover: http://www.happyabout.info/30daybootcamp/life-makeover.php
- The Business Rule Revolution: http://happyabout.info/business-rule-revolution.php
- Happy About Global Software Test Automation: http://www.happyabout.info/globalswtestautomation.php
- Happy About Joint Venturing: http://happyabout.info/jointventuring.php
- Happy About LinkedIn for Recruiting: http://happyabout.info/linkedin4recruiting.php
- Happy About Website Payments with PayPal http://happyabout.info/paypal.php
- Happy About Outsourcing: http://happyabout.info/outsourcing.php

Contents

Contents

Chapter

1 Introduction

What is it about some companies? Year in, year out, their performance just seems to get better and better. Occasionally they stumble, but then come back stronger than ever. They're not hard to find. All you need to do is read the headlines: "GE predicts double-digit growth for 2007." "Apple Tops *Business Week* list of Innovative Companies." "Southwest Carries More Passengers than Any Other U.S. Airline."

These companies seem to play in a different league than others. It's like watching the New York Yankees play a minor league baseball team.

In addition to being easy to find, the qualities that make these big league players successful are easy to define. They're fast-moving, aligned, proactive and innovative. We would also call them "intelligent." They make effective decisions, they anticipate or create market trends and they optimize all their resources, especially the unique skills of each individual. They use information technology skillfully.

So, we know who these winners are and what qualities they have. The next obvious question is: "How did they get there?" Or, perhaps more to the point: "How can my business get there?" This is what this book is about. It's about how to create an *Intelligent Business*, one that is smart, innovative and profitable. What we're offering is not incremental change, but transformation at the organizational level.

We encourage you to aim high. The concepts in this book are designed to create a business fully capable of operating in any league. A careful look at highly successful companies shows that they won't settle for anything less than excellence in all their activities. Why should you?

How

So, how does one go about creating an intelligent business? For most companies, it's by a process of trial and error. Highly successful companies have arrived at their own unique methods of reaching the top. These businesses may have succeeded, but the path of trial and error is littered with failures and also-rans. In today's demanding business environment, this path is no longer a viable option.

What we're offering here is a guidebook to creating an organization that employs all its resources in an intelligent manner. We have developed a set of guiding principles called the Ladder of Business Intelligence. As an organization adopts and employs these principles, the Ladder becomes a framework around which a business can grow its intelligence.

This is a step-by-step process, as you can see from the diagram of the Ladder. As an organization climbs higher, it employs all its resources more skillfully.

Let's take a brief look at the various steps on the Ladder.

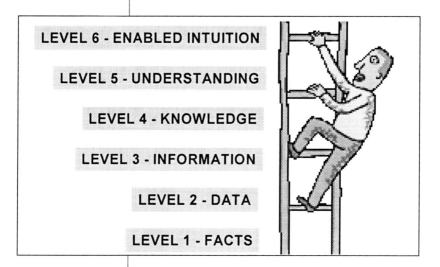

LEVEL 6 - ENABLED INTUITION

LEVEL 5 - UNDERSTANDING

LEVEL 4 - KNOWLEDGE

LEVEL 3 - INFORMATION

LEVEL 2 - DATA

LEVEL 1 - FACTS

Level 1. **Facts** represent the recording of an event or measure in the "real" world. Imagine a bulletin board with a number of post-it notes. Each of these notes contains certain facts, but they are totally unorganized. If you want to find facts in a certain category – say, automobiles for sale – you will have to search across the entire board.

Level 2. **Data** is composed of organized facts. Imagine that the bulletin board has now been organized into categories: each note has been placed in a labeled section of the board. Your search for a car has now become simpler, but you still have to search through all the postings for autos.

Level 3. | **Information** is data that has been organized to answer a specific question. For example, there are now a number of Web sites where you can fill in the details about the kind of car you want. The site will then present you with a number of choices from sellers. Forget the post-it notes. Because your search has been automated, it has become much simpler and less time consuming. You now have the information you need to make a good decision on buying a car. Translated to a business environment, it means freedom from searching through scores of spreadsheets for bits of data. Instead, the information technology organizes facts and data according to the questions you need answered. A sales manager, for instance, might have the total sales for the last three months available on her display device. This enables her to view trends and take action accordingly.

Level 4. | **Knowledge** consists of information and the derived rules on how to use the information. It includes best practices and knowledge about trends and behavior.

Level 5. | **Understanding** is knowledge that is shared. It refers to the alignment that occurs throughout an organization when company visions, strategies, and rules are shared and understood at all levels.

Level 6. | **Enabled Intuition** is a higher level of understanding that facilitates decision makers to intuitively choose the right course of action that will benefit the business in any situation. With enabled intuition decision making is refined to an art.

The majority of businesses operate at Levels 1 and 2, with people struggling to gather facts and data and interpret them. Not only do they have to search for the data, they then have to organize it into a form that allows to them make an effective business decision.

At Level 3, the task of sorting through the data and organizing is performed by the information system. The information is then displayed on command to the individual that needs it.

We define Information as something that enables an intelligent decision and subsequent action.

As an example, at Level 2, the sales manager might have a figure for sales to Customer A for the month of August. This is a potentially useful piece of data, but there is no business context in which to place it. At Level 3, the manager is presented with sales to Customer A for the last three months, showing a decline during that period. This automated organization of data – this information – enables the manager to take immediate action.

As an organization becomes more skilled at turning facts and data into useful information, decision making is enhanced at all levels. Each individual is able to act more swiftly and with greater certainty that his or her decisions will move the company in the direction of its objectives. In addition, since information is disseminated among all players in any business process or project, communication and collaboration are also enhanced. This means, for example, that our sales manager will have plenty of informed people ready to help her address the situation with Customer A.

In an intelligent business, the right information is delivered to the right people at the right time.

Information as Answers

If we can agree that having key information delivered to your display device is a powerful asset, the next question might be: How does one create that key information? In the Ladder framework, the answer is, by asking the right questions.

Most of us have been trained in school to answer questions. Information is given to us and then we are asked to answer questions about this information. Getting good at asking questions, however, can be a powerful way of learning. These should be insightful questions – the kind that produce significant answers. Asking insightful questions is one of the key steps to creating an intelligent business.

Later in the book, we'll devote an entire section to the process of asking the right questions. Right now, let's summarize that process.

At a certain point in the Ladder framework, each decision maker is asked to clarify his or her business role, with the help of his or her team. What are the specific objectives, activities and processes that this role is accountable for? What processes are involved in reaching his goals?

Then, he is asked to formulate five to ten questions that he needs answered in order to perform his job better. What information does he need to appear on his display device every day, every week or every month?

Our sales manager, for example, would probably ask for a total monthly sales figure – a summary of regional sales figures. She would also like to see how this figure compares to previous months, as well as how it compares to projections made at the beginning of the fiscal year. Access to figures like these will give her the information she needs to make intelligent, timely decisions.

After each decision maker has formulated his or her questions, the Information Technology experts choose the right software applications to provide the correct information views for each business role.

Creating Good Information

Good information is created by implementing models that produce useful answers to insightful questions. The value of the resulting information is directly proportional to the business impact of the decision that has been enabled.

Therefore, we must all become very good at *asking the right questions*. If we ask the right questions, profits will follow. If we ask trivial questions, then the resulting information will have little impact on the business.

This view of information as an answer to a question is simple, yet powerful. Many people spend their lives chasing facts and data, not information.

The operational sequence is *Question – Information – Decision (Q-I-D)*. This is the operational decision triangle of power. The objective of a Business Intelligence (BI) team is to partner with the other business units to create the correct information views for making fast and effective business decisions.

The right decision by the right person at the right time is the oil for a smoothly running organization. Information provides correct answers to key questions. If the output from the computer does not answer a key question for you, then it is data and not information. Hence, you need to be focused on creating the correct questions to achieve your goals.

Creating a New Organizational Nervous System

The creation and management of information is essentially the nervous system of an organization. A nervous system – whether biological or organizational – has a number of tasks. Among the most important are:

- Reporting key events in the external environment and filtering out nonessential data
- Monitoring the internal environment
- Deciding on responses to external and internal conditions
- Coordinating the organism or organization to act
- Creating a knowledge base for future action

Speed and focus are the keys to successful reporting and coordinated action. Speed, because both the natural world and the business world require rapid responses, and focus because it's necessary to filter out extraneous data and present only critical information.

When an organization is able to create, retrieve, store and share information effectively, a better organizational nervous system has been created. A successful system enables effective business decisions, seamless communication, proactive management of processes and projects, the creation of a knowledge base and real organizational alignment.

Nervous Systems

The creation, retrieval, storage and dissemination of information make up the nervous system of an organization. The Ladder provides a framework for a new organizational nervous system – one that more closely resembles the exquisite systems of humans and animals.

In nature, survival depends on the ability to respond to an opportunity or a threat in a rapid and coordinated manner. This means that the control and feedback between the brain and the body must be almost instantaneous. For example, a rabbit escaping from a fox must speedily coordinate its entire body to evade the predator.

A business needs to imitate these neural feedback loops. It has to have a nervous system that smoothly connects a strategy to daily operations and decisions, just as the biological system coordinates the different organs and limbs of the body. When every business unit is aware of the overall direction and strategy of the company, then each decision they make will be, by definition, intelligent and aligned. These decisions will also be swift.

Luckily, these abilities do not need to evolve over millennia, but can be acquired in a relatively short time. An organizational nervous system is a combination of human and machine intelligence acting in concert. The Ladder provides a framework for this happy collaboration.

People, Process and Technology

When the new nervous system is in operation, a business is able to optimize all its resources, especially the most valuable ones like:

- *People.* An intelligent business employs human intelligence to its fullest capacity. People are skilled at envisioning and figuring out how to make the visions come true. When they are relieved of doing work better done by machines (like searching for and organizing data), people are free to exercise their intelligence and creativity.

- *Process.* An intelligent business has a first-rate infrastructure. Transforming visions into competitive products and services requires seamless, but flexible, business processes.

- *Technology.* Smart businesses make optimal use of business technology. These businesses use the right information to enable effective decision making, communication and collaboration.

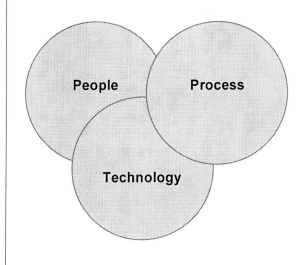

People, Process and Technology: Here's a trio that you will see throughout this book. The Ladder framework enables organizations to streamline these key resources – their People, Processes and Technologies – and optimize the level of automation in the creation and use of information. This creates a powerful infrastructure able to employ all its resources in bringing ideas to the marketplace smoothly and efficiently.

The key points in the three circles are the areas where they intersect. These are the places where People, Process and Technology are operating in synch. When this happens, two more qualities of an intelligent organization can emerge:

- *Proactive*. An intelligent business is able to observe the progress of its processes and projects. This enables its decisions to be proactive rather than reactive in correcting and enhancing business processes.

- *Innovative*. A business employing all its resources in an intelligent manner is able to stay ahead of its markets and its competitors. It encourages and enables innovation at every level of the organization. It is never complacent, but always looking to the future.

By the end of this book, you should be very familiar with these qualities – and understand why they are key to the success of any business.

In addition, you may discover that you possess new skills:

- *Diagnosis*. You may find yourself able to evaluate the level of intelligence of your business and others. Are your decision-makers skilled at retrieving and employing key information to make smart decisions? Are you able to act quickly on the decisions? Is there general understanding and support of the corporate vision and goals? What about your competitors: what level have they achieved?

- *Next Steps.* Once you have diagnosed the strengths and weaknesses of your company, the next steps are likely to become clear. For example, if your evaluation places your business intelligence system at Levels 1 and 2, you will understand what you need to do to enable it to reach Level 3 where it will generate useful information.

- *How to proceed.* When you reach the final page of this book, you will have an overview of how to ascend to the top of the Ladder. In other words, you will understand what it takes to create a successful, intelligent business.

Step by Step, Chapter by Chapter

It's important to note that the creation of an intelligent business involves a step-by-step process. The sequential nature of the ascent up the Ladder is what makes it effective. Certain steps simply will not work unless the previous steps have been mastered. This book is laid out so that the sequence is clear.

Each Chapter Answers Key Questions

Chapters 1 and 2 answer the questions: What and why? What is this Ladder? Why should I be interested? What can it do for me? In Chapter 2, we'll take a look at two successful, highly intelligent businesses and discuss how the Ladder can help your business operate in the same league.

Chapters 3,4, 5 and 6 answer: How? How do you go about changing the way a company functions? How do you optimize the key resources of a business: its People, Processes and Technology?

Chapter 7 answers the question: What are the results? What have we attained? What are the differences between organizations at Levels 1 and 2 and those at Levels 3 and up?

Chapter 8 answers: Is all this absolutely necessary? In the 21st century, yes! The demanding economic environment, rigorous competition and regulatory requirements mean that a business must employ all its resources to their fullest extent.

Finally, Chapter 9 answers: What about the future? Will this Ladder framework continue to help us to grow and innovate?

The Intelligent Business

Our goal in this book is to describe the creation of an Intelligent Business. The way this is achieved is by ascending each step of the Ladder of Business Intelligence. This carefully arranged process will enable a business to attain its goals and fulfill its true potential. A business that functions at Levels 3 and up essentially plays in a different league than those companies stuck at Levels 1 and 2.

Let's look at the key qualities of an intelligent business.

The Intelligent Business:

- Employs human intelligence at its fullest capacity
- Employs business intelligence optimally

- Uses quality information to enable effective decision making, communication and robust cross functional collaboration
- Employs the above three capabilities to create seamless business processes and a robust infrastructure
- Encourages innovation at every level of the organization
- Is always proactive, never complacent

This is the Intelligent Business – one in which People, Process and Technology – the most valuable assets in any business – work together to create a world-class enterprise. Why should you be satisfied with anything less?

NOTE "We introduce a fictionalized company in Chapter 3 to illustrate the points of the Ladder throughout the book. Tom is the expert on the Ladder from that company and we summarize the chapters using Tom's Takeaways."

Tom's Takeaways: FAQs about the Ladder of Business Intelligence

Q. Are the Ladder methods difficult to implement?
A. Not when they're accomplished gradually. People who have done it say that it's usually much more difficult to continue conducting business in the old ways.

Q. Do I need to take an advanced course in Information Technology to understand the Ladder?

A. No. The beauty of this methodology is that managers can understand the larger picture and the specific cost benefits without understanding the technologies involved. These are left to the IT specialists.

Q. What kind of organization is a good candidate for the Ladder?

A. Any organization – business or non-business – large or small – that feels the need to grow and change. Whether you come from aspiration or desperation, the end results can be the same.

Q. Can the Ladder be employed for a single business unit?

A. Absolutely. We have worked with divisions of large corporations. Implementing the Ladder in one sector allows managers to view its advantages. They can then decide if it's right for the entire organization.

Q. Is all this going to cost an arm and a leg?

A. Generally, no. While the costs will vary for different organizations, most of the resources, like the people, are already there. And because the necessary software applications are carefully tailored to the needs of each business role, the cost of the technology is minimized. In addition, the increased efficiency and more rapid cycle time to action are soon reflected in the bottom line.

2 Best Companies, Best Practices

The Intelligent Organization

Our goal is to help you build an intelligent business – one that makes excellent decisions based on the best information. But before we get into exactly how to accomplish this, it might be useful to look at the qualities of intelligent companies. This is what this chapter is about.

Instead of simply listing these qualities, we're going to look at how a couple of smart, successful firms conduct their business. Then, at the end of the chapter, we'll review their special attributes and discuss how the Ladder can instill these qualities in your business.

These companies have essentially arrived at their own version of the People-Process-Technology framework described by the Ladder. Through trial and error, skillful management and perseverance, they have created organizations with the same attributes as those that have adopted the Ladder framework. But could they have accomplished this faster and more easily by following – say – a recipe?

A Recipe for Success

Have you ever tasted a cake baked by Julia Child? Probably not. But luckily, this master chef devoted much of her life to bringing her recipes and techniques to the rest of us. Through her many cookbooks, her delightful television shows and her cooking school, she made her delicious recipes available to millions.

Because of this, there's a very good chance that you've tasted a cake based on a recipe by Child. She had a knack for making her recipes so simple and straightforward that even an ordinary cook can make a prizewinning cake.

It's interesting to note that the ingredients for these recipes are not unusual: just your usual flour, eggs, butter, sugar, milk, etc. What makes her recipes special are the processes: how to beat the eggs to a certain consistency, the exact time to add the milk, how long and at what temperature to bake the cake – all these simple processes, when followed in the right sequence, produce the memorable dessert.

This is what we're aiming to do here. We're essentially giving you a *recipe for success*. We have put together certain procedures and processes that, when followed in a logical sequence, can result in prizewinning companies. Like Julia's recipes, these processes are not difficult to follow and most of them will be familiar to you.

The beauty of the Ladder framework is that you don't need legendary leaders to bring a company to greatness. All you need are normal people willing to perform a certain set of procedures and processes. This framework will all be laid out in following chapters.

But first, let's look at how two highly su firms conduct their businesses.

Fun as a Company Policy

Southwest Airlines Flight 55 from San Diego to Portland had been delayed for over an hour. Some of the passengers gazed out gloomily at the rainy tarmac, others tried to read, mothers soothed fussy children. Suddenly, there was a fanfare of music on the intercom and everyone looked up to see one of the flight attendants with a tiara on her head and a red boa around her neck. Two other attendants stood on either side of her, also with boas.

"Welcome to Southwest Club 55!" announced the tiarad attendant and commenced a dance routine with the other attendants. The women moved up and down the aisles, swaying to the music, swishing their boas over the passengers and tickling the children with the feathers. By the end of the routine, passengers were cheering and clapping and children were trying to imitate the dance in the aisles.

Everyone has a favorite Southwest story – like the attendant that announced: "Ladies and gentlemen, if you wish to smoke, the smoking section on this airplane is on the wing and if you can light 'em, you can smoke 'em."

All in a day's work at Southwest. But there is method behind this madness. The employees who make you laugh are seeing to it that your flight is enjoyable, even memorable. Of course, you want to get from San Diego to Portland quickly and safely, but hey, let's have a little fun on the way. And just maybe, when you're choosing airlines for your next flight, you'll remember that you had a good time on Southwest.

The fun is not confined to the aircraft. At corporate headquarters in Memphis, the nameplate on the receptionist's desk reads, "Director of First Impressions." A bobble-headed doll of the CEO sits on the red boa-decorated desk while an oxygen mask hangs from the ceiling. A "Culture Committee" organizes fundraisers to pay for parties and celebrations throughout the year. Practical jokes are played on everyone, including senior executives.

The fun tends to build a sense of family among employees, reminding them that they're part of a special company. In 2005, Southwest received 260,000 resumes for 2,700 positions. *Fortune* magazine has rated it number three among America's ten most admired companies.

Here's a statement from the company Web site: "The mission of Southwest Airlines is dedication to the highest quality of Customer Service delivered with a sense of warmth, friendliness, individual pride, and Company Spirit. Employees will be provided the same concern, respect, and caring attitude within the organization that they are expected to share externally with every Southwest Customer. Creativity and innovation are encouraged for improving the effectiveness of Southwest Airlines."

A Winning Business Model

Simplicity is the name of the Southwest business model. For example, because Southwest only flies Boeing 737s, repair and maintenance time is minimized. No seats are reserved and food service is generally confined to a soft drink and a bag of chips. Southwest offers ticketless travel to hold down back-office costs and operates its own reservation system. 67% of its reservations in 2005 were made online.

The company has achieved the fastest turnaround time in the industry. Aircraft are cleaned, checked out, luggage is loaded and crews are ready to go in record time. Southwest's reputation for fun can obscure this fine attention to process. This is an airline that knows what it's doing.

The airline began service in 1971 and now has more than 32,000 employees managing 3,100 flights a day. They carried over 88 million passengers in 2005 through 60 cities in 30 states – more than any other airline. Since 1987, Southwest has maintained the fewest overall Customer complaints as published in the Department of Transportation's *Air Travel Consumer Report*. In 2005, Southwest ranked first in Customer Satisfaction. The carrier has enjoyed 33 straight profitable years amid the airline industry's ups and downs (mostly downs, recently).

Level 5: Understanding

In the framework of the Ladder, we would say that Southwest has reached Level 5 – the level of *Understanding*. At this level, there is general understanding throughout the organization of the company vision and of the strategies needed to achieve that vision. Each person at Southwest knows that his or her job is to relate to customers in a friendly, helpful manner – and to add some fun whenever possible.

There is first-rate collaboration among all parties in conducting each flight and turning the aircraft around in record time. Indeed, that magic word, *alignment*, is present in the way employees conduct all the business of the company.

This is a prime example of Level 5 Understanding at work.

The Joys of Smallness

Southwest illustrates a certain key point better than any other company. The people at Southwest know that business is ultimately about satisfying *customers* – and doing it efficiently enough that you make money. All the other things that a business does, like setting goals, building processes, having a satisfied workforce or a culture that encourages change, are simply means to accomplishing this primary goal.

In small businesses, this is a no-brainer. Everyone knows that their job depends on pleasing customers. The success of each employee is closely connected to the success of the company. Another way of saying this is that the vested interests of everyone coincide, from management to front-line workers.

Small companies have other qualities that make them fast-moving and efficient. Because everyone is in shouting distance of each other, information is easily disseminated and discussed. Collaboration happens naturally because everyone knows who is responsible for what.

Spirits tend to be high in fast-growing firms. People feel that they are valued members of a successful community and know that they will be recognized and rewarded for their efforts. They share their creative ideas and work long hours. All this results in quick response to customer demands and a rapid cycle time to market.

As organizations grow, however, they begin to subdivide into numbers of functional departments, both to gain the benefits of specialization and to create units of manageable size. This division tends to encourage each department to develop its own unique culture and language: decision making can become fragmented, and both information gathering and monitoring progress become specialized.

In this atmosphere, managers often begin to work for the goals of their functional units, instead of for company-wide objectives. Organizational silos are created, turf is protected, and visions that encompass the whole enterprise can get lost in interdepartmental friction. Employees may perceive their vested interests as simply retaining their job or pleasing their superiors.

Communication is often thwarted by these diverse departmental cultures, as well as by geographical distances and the sheer number of people. The free exchange of information vital to organizational alignment and productive collaboration may be lost.

So the questions we're asking here are: how to maintain the special qualities of a small company while leveraging the advantages of size and resources of a large firm? How to keep people focused on pleasing customers? How to keep communication vital and pertinent so that collaboration comes naturally? How to align the vested interests of the various business units with the goals of the organization? How to keep people motivated and happy to come to work?

These are the kind of questions that the Ladder of Business Intelligence addresses. We want it all: the small firm's ability to move fast, communicate easily and create alignment coupled with the power and resources of a large, growing company.

These are the same questions that firms like Southwest and other highly successful companies have dealt with as they grew into large corporations.

But could they have done it more rapidly and easily by following the Ladder framework? Probably. Could you bake a better cake more quickly by following one of Julia Child's recipes instead of starting from scratch? Probably.

"Whatever it Takes" In the popular film, Cast Away, Tom Hanks plays a FedEx agent who is marooned on an island when his transport plane crashes in the Pacific Ocean. After five years, he manages to escape the island and is rescued from the ocean clinging to a package. One of the last scenes shows Hanks delivering the beat-up package to the addressee.

Fiction, to be sure, but FedEx has built a reputation on real performance. When you send a package with FedEx, you can be reasonably sure that it will arrive in the time frame you choose. In the U.S., the marketing tag line is, "Relax, it's FedEx." In Europe, it's, "Whatever it takes," referring to the efforts that individual employees will go to ensure that the package arrives on time. Like Southwest, employees are proud of their roles in this process and see clearly that their success is closely tied to the success of the company.

The Beauty of Automation

In addition to delivering on time, FedEx makes it possible for you to track the progress of the delivery online. Out of several million packages per day, the FedEx information system knows where each one is at any given moment. The system they have created can also give you the estimated time of delivery.

The folks at FedEx approached this from the angle of the customer. They asked, "What does the customer need to know at any given moment?" Customers have a finite list of questions about their transaction, like, "Hey, where's my shipment? When is it going to get here? Is it safe?" They realized that if they could identify this list of questions and develop a system to answer them, then they wouldn't need operators sitting there 24/7.

Imagine the enormous workforce it would take to track each package manually and answer customer questions. Now imagine these people doing other, more productive, activities and you can see the beauty of having your key questions answered by information technology. At this very minute, these people are probably thinking up ways that FedEx can improve its services and continue to outrun the competition.

This illustration can be compared to the capabilities enabled by the Ladder framework. The Ladder team asks that each decision maker in a company decide on a few key questions that he or she needs answered in a given time frame. The answers to these questions – accessible on a display device – contain information that allows managers to make smart business decisions. The FedEx technology allows customers to get answers to key questions while technology in the Ladder framework enables managers to receive answers to their key questions.

Facts, Data, and Information

The FedEx system gives you certain facts and data about your shipment that you may need. For example, if a package containing important documents has been delayed because of a storm, you will want to know the fact that the package is safe and undamaged. But the system will also give you a new estimated time of arrival (ETA). This might allow you to reschedule a meeting that involve the documents

Take note that this ETA is in the category of Information – something that enables an informed decision. At the level of Facts, you would discover only that your package is safe and sitting on a loading dock in Denver. At the level of Data, you would learn that your package originated in Miami, was rerouted to Dallas to avoid a storm and is presently in Denver. While these bits might ease your mind, neither of them

Chapter 2: Best Companies, Best Practices

would allow you to make any intelligent decisions. Only the ETA contains the *information* necessary for you to take action and reschedule your meeting.

Priorities at FedEx

The corporate philosophy at FedEx is summarized as "People-Service-Profit." Founder and CEO Frederick Smith states that: "When people are placed first they will provide the highest possible service, and profits will follow." From the start, he vowed to make employees an integral part of the decision-making process. As an indication of its regard for its employees, all company planes are named after the children of employees.

The People goal, as stated on the company Web site, is to create an environment where employees feel secure enough to take risks and become innovative in pursuing quality, service and customer satisfaction. Service refers to the quality goal of "100% customer satisfaction, 100% of the time." Then, if the people and service goals have been met, a corporate Profit should result.

Profits have indeed resulted from this formula, growing steadily over the years. For the quarter ending August 31, 2006, for instance, FedEx reported revenues of $8.54 billion, up 11% from the previous year. Net income was $475 million, up 40% from the previous year. During the past ten years, FedEx has expanded its range of services by acquiring several other successful delivery firms. From 2000 to 2006, its stock tripled in value while the overall market stumbled or remained flat.

Intelligent Businesses

We view both Southwest and FedEx as intelligent businesses. They operate with sound common sense and great attention to the alignment of people, process and technology.

Both firms start with a clear vision. In our opinion, setting a clear direction and broadcasting it to both employees and the public is the first smart thing to do. Will FedEx ever reach its goal of 100% customer satisfaction 100% of the time? Probably not, but everyone in the company knows this goal and strives to reach it. We see this vision as helping to create internal alignment and a company-wide focus on customer satisfaction. Like Southwest, we would say that FedEx has also achieved Level 5 on the Ladder.

Both Southwest and FedEx have a strong dedication to their employees. Both seem to realize that real customer satisfaction can only be achieved when all employees see this as their main job. In this way, both firms have held on to their small company origins, when pleasing each and every customer was a matter of survival.

There are plenty of studies that show that increased revenues result when employee satisfaction rises. Of course, employees want good pay, benefits and job security. But our model companies go far beyond these norms. Southwest says it best when it states that "employees will be provided the same concern, respect, and caring attitude within the organization that they are expected to share externally with every Southwest Customer."

Once you have an inspiring vision that everyone understands and you have the support of your employees, the other aspects of success are likely to follow much more easily. For example, our two poster companies also excel at changing with the times. During the thirty-plus years of their existence, the economic landscape has altered dramatically, but they have shown continual resilience and growth. They are also masters at employing information technology, thus freeing their employees to concentrate on building new strategies to confound the competition.

Perhaps we should give these firms "Honorary Ladder Degrees." By employing their own individual methods and cultures, they have attained the higher levels of the Ladder without even going through the specific methodology!

Intelligence

In the Ladder framework, the alignment of vision, strategies, processes and information is what creates intelligence and seamless collaboration. The intelligent business functions at Level 3 and up. Businesses operating at these higher levels of information and intelligence have a distinct competitive advantage over businesses that are still functioning at Levels 1 and 2.

In the intelligent business, the right information is delivered to the right people at the right time. The goal is an organization where effective business decisions are based on quality information and vigorous collaboration. These decisions, in turn, enable a business to be proactive in its ability to envision new markets, new products and future economic environments.

> Effective decisions then lead to the seamless translation of a vision into an actual product or service. In this case, "seamless" implies a shorter time to market with less expense, as well as higher quality products with greater profit margins. This is the intelligent business at work.

Building Success

We've focused on just two companies in this chapter. We want to make it clear, however, that other successful firms we have worked with possess the same, or similar, qualities. In addition, the "great" companies portrayed in Jim Collins' *Good to Great* possess these qualities. A clear and inspiring vision, a respect for employees' needs and input, a passionate attention to process and the skillful use of information technology are qualities seen in most highly successful businesses.

It has been our experience that the Ladder of Business Intelligence builds these qualities directly into the DNA of an organization. In the following four chapters, we're going to demonstrate exactly how this is accomplished. Our goal is always an intelligent business, one in which good decisions are based on quality information and robust collaboration.

In this kind of business, the right information is delivered to the right people at the right time. An understanding of vision and strategies creates alignment at all levels. These abilities enable an organization – large or small – to move with the speed and the certainty of an athlete.

Tom's Takeaways

What do successful organizations excel at?

1. Formulating a Vision. Where are we going? What are we passionate about? What do we do best?

2. Communicating their vision so that all employees feel an ownership of the vision and the strategies.

3. Valuing their employees: Paying attention to what they need and encouraging their input.

4. A passionate attention to processes – especially core processes.

5. Listening to and communicating with all stakeholders.

6. Steady improvement. Ability to change.

7. Excellence in creating and managing information. This enables intelligent decisions.

8. Rapid cycle times to information and action.

9. Seamless cross-functional collaboration.

Tom's Takeaways #2

Business Relevancy of the LOBI Framework

The LOBI framework consists of the LOBI six step maturity model (the Ladder) and the Circle of Success, as shown on page 48, which reinforce each other. While the Ladder represents the meta framework, the Circle of Success represents the operational steps that an organization must execute to climb the Ladder.

Each step up the Ladder is dependent on the step below. Hence, this is an ordered climb and evolution. One must be able to load all the accurate facts (S1) about the business entities of interest before one can move to the data step (S2). The Ladder steps can be summarized as follows:

- S1 The *fact* step is simply the foundation – a business attains this step by virtue of being in business and gathering facts about its business entities of interest.

- S2 At the *data* step, a business gains efficiency and flexibility in referring to facts about its customers/employees/partners. Data enables other applications and provides economies of scale for support costs across systems via reusability.

- S3 At the *information* step, a business becomes capable of taking effective action to counter challenges or identify new opportunities. Business roles link information needs to key performance indicators (KPIs) for each role. Business roles become more effective as information is utilized.

- S4 The *knowledge* step represents the leverage that a business has about its clients/markets/partners. This is the step where a business gains most value from information by reusing methods, concepts and experience across operating units.

- S5 The *understanding* step impacts the effectiveness that the firm has in the marketplace over the long run. Companies that have reached this step tend to outlast competition, because they are beginning to gain an insight into a customer's mind and see opportunities before their competition does. At this step, a company is also solving strategic problems through worldwide collaboration.

- S6 The *enabled intuition* step is where "out of the box" solutions are created. Attaining S6 assists with enabled intuition. Once understanding of several business domains has been attained, one has a higher probability of observing inter-domain opportunities.

Step 4 in the Circle of Success utilizes the Business Role Intelligence Analysis (BRIA) tool, which identifies the business questions and entities that must be represented in our system. BRIA allows us to define the processes necessary to generate the information to answer the questions. A successful creation of a BRIA allows one to execute the remaining steps of the Circle of Success. BRIA is the tool that connects the people, process, and technology triplet to products, services, customers and any other business entity of interest.

BRIA allows each business role to define the top ten questions at any of the first three steps of the ladder. However, it is only at S3, the information step, that executives begin receiving the information that they need to make business decisions relevant for their roles. Therefore, S3 is a pivotal step up the ladder. S3 builds on the first two steps and is in turn leveraged by the next two steps. Finally, S6 is enabled by the five steps below it.

The business value of a step can be measured by its LOBI rating which represents the coverage of the questions that must be answered for each business role. The intelligence needs of a step have been completely fulfilled, when you have provided the intelligence to answer all the questions for each business role. For example, if a business role has defined 10 questions at S3, the business role has a LOBI rating of 2.5 when only five of the ten questions have been answered and displayed by the system. To determine an organization's LOBI rating, you take a sum of all of the business role ratings and calculate the average.

When the intelligence system has completed answering all of the questions at S3, you will be ready to move to S4 and capture the best practice rules that you have just created as business rules and define them as knowledge. The identification of the process roadmap in step 5 of the Circle of Success forces collaboration and the migration to S4.

As you traverse the steps of the Circle of Success, the excitement throughout the entire enterprise will continue to build as each business role will see their cycle time to information/knowledge continue to decline and as a consequence allow each one of them to reduce their cycle time to action!

3 Visions and Strategies

In the last chapter, we talked about success. The Ladder of Business Intelligence is essentially a recipe for success – a series of processes and procedures that, when followed in a logical sequence, lead to success.

In this chapter, we begin the tour through the Ladder framework. The first steps in this sequence are to create an inspiring company vision and a realistic mission statement. These are critical steps because they set the direction for the entire organization.

Imagine, if you will, a voyage on which the first officer gets the destination wrong. When the ship steams off from port – in the wrong direction – *every subsequent decision made on the ship is, by definition, wrong.* That's the importance of the company vision.

Southwest Airlines provides us with a superb example of a company vision: "Dedication to the highest quality of Customer Service delivered with a sense of warmth, friendliness, individual pride, and Company Spirit." This statement (which is also the company's mission statement) tells employees what is expected of them and it does so in inspiring language. It also tells customers, other stakeholders and the rest of the world what Southwest Airlines is all about.

Most companies have a vision statement and a mission statement. The vision statement is concise, timeless and inclusive enough to speak to employees customers, investors and the general public. It explains *why* the company exists. The mission statement is a very concise statement of business strategy – *what* do we do and *how* do we do it.

For example, at FedEx, "Leading the way" is the vision statement. The mission statement gets more specific: "FedEx Corporation will produce superior financial returns for its shareowners by providing high value-added logistics, transportation and related information services through focused operating companies."

This chapter lays out the best ways to get the company vision and mission right. It also begins to demonstrate how this high-level envisioning can be translated into each strategy and each key business process. To make this description more vivid, we're going to tell the story of a mid-size company that is employing the Ladder to reshape itself. The problems faced by this fictionalized company mimic those of the numerous companies we have worked with, both large and small.

Natural Bounty

Natural Bounty is a chain of 110 natural foods store. In 2004, the company made an initial public offering of stock and, over the next two years, used the proceeds to acquire fifty additional stores.

Natural Bounty Organization Chart

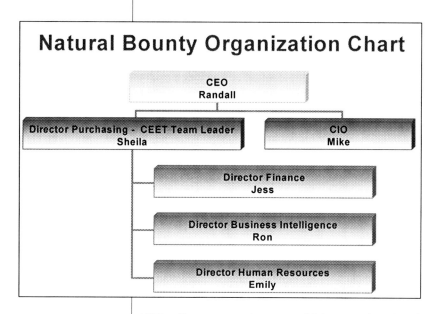

```
                    CEO
                   Randall
        ┌─────────────────┴─────────────────┐
  Director Purchasing - CEET Team Leader        CIO
                Sheila                          Mike
        │
        ├──────── Director Finance
        │              Jess
        │
        ├──────── Director Business Intelligence
        │              Ron
        │
        └──────── Director Human Resources
                       Emily
```

With the new stores, which consisted of individual markets and small chains, came a number of problems. For example, the company must now deal with a myriad of diverse business processes and information technology platforms.

Natural Bounty also needs to standardize its various stores. What can a customer expect when he or she goes into a Natural Bounty store, whether it's in Texas or British Columbia? How are employees expected to act and what products should be common to all stores? What are the company's overall strategies, values and core practices? *And, above all, how can management create a successful business model in an increasingly competitive field?*

The executive management team understands that the company needs to be reinvented. Having nearly doubled in size, Natural Bounty needs a new vision and a winning business model.

The company has engaged a team of three Ladder experts to help with these challenges. The first thing that these experts recommended was the creation of an internal, company team: the Corporate Effectiveness and Efficiency Team or CEET. The individuals on this team were chosen for the scope of their vision. These are people who understand where the company needs to go and what it will take to get it there. They were also chosen for their leadership abilities. These are visionaries who are also movers and shakers, individuals who can influence and inspire others to change.

Here's what the CEET team looks like at Natural Bounty:

- Sheila: Director of Purchasing
- Ron: Director of Information Technology (IT)
- Jess: Director of Finance
- Emily: Director of Human Resources (HR)
- Tom is the head of the Ladder team – a team of experts hired by the company.

* * * * *

Sheila slammed her briefcase down on her desk. She was a short woman, but powerful, as evidenced by the loud slap the leather case made on the wooden desk.

"In my next lifetime, I'm going to be a consultant and go around messing up other people's lives!"

The two men and one woman seated around Sheila's desk looked at each other.

"They call themselves 'experts,' Sheila," ventured a balding man with glasses and gray hair. "'Facilitators.'"

"Yeah, well, they still walk like ducks to me, Ron."

"But..."

"Look," said Sheila, "I'm interested in three things around here. Getting my job done, getting paid and getting home to my husband and children. I do my job well – I earn my pay – and I don't see why I need someone to tell me how to do it better. I mean, do they know more about my job than I do?

"Sheila, I have to disagree with you." The speaker was a soft-spoken young woman with short brown hair. "You *do* care about organics and the company. I've heard you."

"Yes, Emily, yes, we all care about this natural stuff. But where has it gotten us? I joined a small chain of markets interested in the best natural products. Then, all of a sudden, we do a public stock offering and management uses the proceeds to buy fifty more stores and we're twice as big. Now, we're a big messy chain with more stores than we can deal with. I've just spent the last two months visiting twenty-five of these stores – and, believe me when I say that things are messy."

"I know Sheila," Emily sighed. "A lot of us are not happy with our new company. Some people have quit, others have considered it. But I do want to make it work – and I think we can."

The second man in the room spoke up. He was tall and young, with his dark hair tied back in a ponytail. "This is why we need these people, Sheila." He spoke earnestly, with a slight southern accent. "We've inherited dozens of different processes and different information platforms with these acquisitions. Then, in the stores, there are different operating procedures, different products – no unity, no standards. That's what these people are here to help us with."

Sheila leaned back in her chair and ran a hand through her short, blond hair. "Okay, Jess, suppose I grant you that we could use some help. Tell me then why our great leader made me the head of their implementation team. I'm in Operations, not IT. And Emily here is in HR. This should be the job of you IT people. Ron, you're second in command at IT."

Ron leaned forward. "CEO Randall asked you to head up this team because we need to do a lot more than just bring up some new technology."

"Explain."

Ron leaned back and crossed his legs. "Let me start by giving you a little background. Do you know the difficulty with acquiring new technology?"

"It doesn't work?" asked Sheila.

"Yes, that is often the problem. But why doesn't it work? These systems can cost hundreds of thousands, often millions. But when they're up and running – if they get that far – many of them don't produce what management wants. Why?"

"I give up," said Sheila. "Why?"

"Because management fails to communicate to us IT folks what they really need. They tell us, 'Go find a system that will help this company grow.' Or, 'Get the latest Enterprise Resource Planning system and make it work for us.' The thing is, they don't know what they need."

Jess raised his hand. "If I may, Ron? What Ron is saying is that there's a major disconnect in communication between the executives, the IT department and the business units. This is not just here – it's happens all over the business world. The executives don't know what the technology has to offer – and, even though this is changing – most IT people don't have the business expertise to understand what the company needs to operate and grow. So, because of this disconnect, only a small percentage of what technology has to offer is used efficiently enough to enhance performance."

"So," asked Sheila, "what's the solution?"

"Can I explain it to her?" asked Emily. "I'd like to see if I've got it right."

"Go for it," said Ron.

"So, Sheila, this is what I've learned from Tom and the Ladder team: What Ron and his IT team need to know are the questions that we need answered by the technology. You know, what are the five or ten pieces of information that you want to see on your display device – every day, every week or every month?

"That's easy," said Sheila. "I could write down three or four right now."

"Yes, and you could probably come up with more if you focused on it. So what our team is going to do is encourage all the decision makers, the business units, the key business roles to focus on the questions they need answered. 'What information do you want the technology to give you?' Then, that'll give the IT experts something to go on. They can tailor the technology to answer those questions."

Sheila shook her head. "That's it? Just ask some questions? It's too simple."

"There is more to it," said Jess. "The Ladder team has a whole program to create what they call an 'intelligent business.' But where it starts is asking questions – the right questions, mind you. Intelligent questions. As the CEET team, we've got to get good at helping people formulate the kind of smart questions that will give them the key information they need."

"It still seems awfully simple to me," said Sheila. "I mean, if it were that simple, other companies would have done it."

"Some have," said Ron. "Those are the ones that are getting the best out of their people, processes and technology. Once we get the right information technology, it's going to help tie the company together. We'll be able to communicate smoothly with all our stores and with each other here at headquarters. What you need to know will be available on your display device instead of having to struggle with finding bits of data on spreadsheets."

Sheila leaned back and looked at the ceiling, then back at Jess. "So, we're going to get the information we need by figuring out what questions we need answered. That sounds good... but if questions are the answer, what questions do we need to ask first?"

"That's easy, said Jess. "We need to ask where we're going – what's our vision for the company. Like, are we going after Whole Foods or are we going to be a bigger version of our great small business model?"

"Now wait a minute," protested Emily. "You're talking about starting at the top with the company vision. I thought this Ladder thing started at the bottom. You know, climbing up from Facts and Data to Information and so on. Ron just told us that we're heading toward getting our questions answered by the technology instead of sifting through data on spreadsheets. So why don't we start with our questions?"

"Good question, Em," said Jess. "The answer is that the company vision and goals are going to help us formulate our questions. You know, you want to know where we're heading, overall and in the near future. Suppose one of the company goals is to improve the customer shopping experience in all of our stores. HR is going to be right in the middle of that because it involves the front line employees. You see what I mean?"

Emily nodded. "Okay, I get that. To ask the right questions, we have to know where we're going. But we've been working on our vision for the last six months. We've been questioning as many customers as we could about the kind of store they want. We've had employee input, executive meetings, middle manager meetings..."

Ron interrupted. "Well, we're not going after Whole Foods," he announced. "I have the company vision and the mission statement right here." He pulled two sheets of paper out of his briefcase.

"Those are the vision and the mission statements?" exclaimed Emily. "After six months, that's all there is?"

"Vision and mission statements need to be short," said Ron. "They're distilled and then distilled again. Want to hear them?"

"Do we want to hear them?" asked Sheila, sarcastically. "Go!"

Ron cleared his throat dramatically. "Here's the vision:

"'Natural Bounty will achieve sustained growth by setting a new standard of excellence in customer service and natural products.'

"And the mission statement:

"'Natural Bounty is dedicated to providing our customers with the highest quality organic foods and health products. Our goal is to serve our customers and our communities while preserving the natural environment that provides us with its bounty.

"'At Natural Bounty, quality will always prevail over quantity. Every store is committed to providing the best in customer service and education in a pleasant, friendly atmosphere. Our goal is the ambiance of a neighborhood market contained in a full-service food and natural products store.'"

Emily cheered and clapped and the others smiled and nodded.

"We're going to think small!" said Jess. "We may get big, but we're going to act like we're small."

"Mom and Pop corner grocery stores," said Emily. "Inviting, intimate and friendly – that's us."

$$\star \quad \star \quad \star \quad \star \quad \star$$

Vision as Direction

Natural Bounty now has a clear vision and mission. To all concerned, the company has announced where it plans to go and how it plans to get there. Both stockholders and potential investors now know the direction the company has chosen. Natural Bounty will not try to become another Whole Foods, but will concentrate on its successful niche market. This niche means smaller and fewer stores than Whole Foods, but, nonetheless, stores with all the services shoppers have come to expect in a supermarket.

In addition, employees at every level in every store now understand what is expected of them. It's all laid out in the mission statement: employees are expected to create a friendly ambiance, with plenty of helpful interaction with customers. And this means that customers will come to know what to expect when they go into any Natural Bounty store.

Asking Questions

The folks at Natural Bounty arrived at their company vision and mission statement by asking questions. They questioned everybody: their managers, their front-line employees, their Board of Directors. "What is this company about? Do we want to become very large very quickly, or do we want to aim for quality in our niche market and grow more slowly? They asked their customers, "What kind of shopping experience do you want? What are you looking for in our stores?"

In high level meetings, executives asked more key questions, like, "What are our core strengths? What are our best opportunities? How can we sustain our growth? What are our main challenges?"

In the Ladder framework, asking people to focus on key questions continues throughout the planning process. People at every level are asked what they need to improve their own performance and that of their business unit. For many people, this may be the first time they have really focused on such questions – the first time they have been asked to use their full intelligence to achieve their goals and the goals of the company.

This is why, in Chapter One, we emphasized the waste inherent in many business. The inadequate use of technology is one such waste, but the poor employment of human intelligence is an even greater waste. The Ladder enables better use of both human and artificial intelligence. And it accomplishes this in a framework that aligns each individual business role with the objectives of the organization.

Measuring Progress

Now that Natural Bounty has defined its direction and purpose, it's time to start transforming that vision into workable objectives and realistic goals. These objectives and goals are usually yearly goals that the company defines in order to move towards its vision. Good objectives are ones that can be simply articulated and show a direct relationship to the vision.

Company objectives need to be measurable. For instance, if Natural Bounty has an objective of standardizing the product line in its markets, it must be able to measure how well and how rapidly this is taking place. It must also measure as precisely as possible if this standardization is contributing to the bottom line. Are more products moving off the shelves? Have the new products shown better profit margins? Or does management need to rethink the product line?

The key metrics that most companies look at are related to:

1. Quality of product or service
2. Cycle time to market
3. Revenue, market share
4. Cost/expense/budget

The metrics can show information at a high level, such as revenue per quarter or cost/expense per quarter. They can also zero in on specific revenues from specific products in specific regions.

So we have objectives, goals and metrics for measuring progress. The next step is to look at how things actually get done. In this case, each metric needs to be connected to specific business processes. Eventually, each process will be tied to a specific owner – a business role, or roles, that will take responsibility for its execution. For example, there will be certain people in certain business roles who will own the task of standardizing the product line in Natural Bounty markets. This process will come under the metric of Quality of Product.

The Enterprise Roadmap

At this point, it can be useful to paint a picture. One of the most important things a company can do is put its vision, goals, metrics and key processes into visual form.

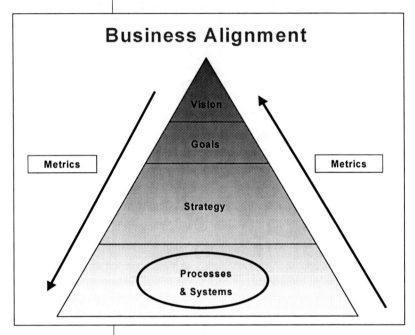

In this case, one picture is worth much more than a thousand words.

Take a look, if you will, at the Enterprise Roadmap below. It depicts the cascading of Vision into Goals and Strategies, then to Key Processes and Strategic Initiatives with the accompanying metrics for moving back and forth.

This picture lays out for all to see where the company plans to go and how it plans to get there. This is a map that can be read from the top down or the bottom up. Either way, it shows how each level is connected to the one above or below.

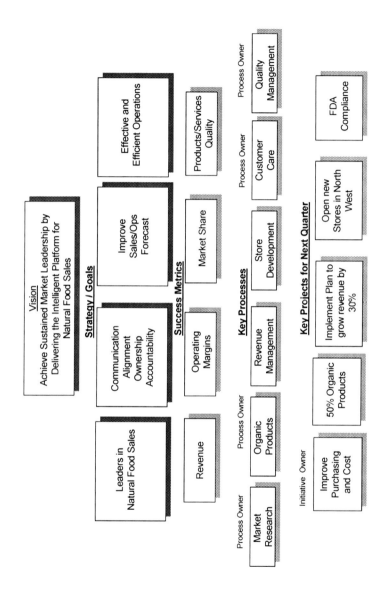

Vision
Achieve Sustained Market Leadership by Delivering the Intelligent Platform for Natural Food Sales

Strategy / Goals

Effective and Efficient Operations

Improve Sales/Ops Forecast

Communication Alignment Ownership Accountability

Leaders in Natural Food Sales

Success Metrics

Products/Services Quality

Market Share

Operating Margins

Revenue

Key Processes

Process Owner
Quality Management

Process Owner
Customer Care

Store Development

Revenue Management

Process Owner
Organic Products

Process Owner
Market Research

Key Projects for Next Quarter

FDA Compliance

Open new Stores in North West

Implement Plan to grow revenue by 30%

50% Organic Products

Initiative Owner
Improve Purchasing and Cost

In Chapter Four, we'll talk further about how the company vision gets translated into action. We'll discuss the Key Processes and how each one acquires its owner. We'll also look at the ways in which each these processes might be improved. If the Ladder is about raising the intelligence of an organization by asking key questions, which questions will the process owners have to answer?

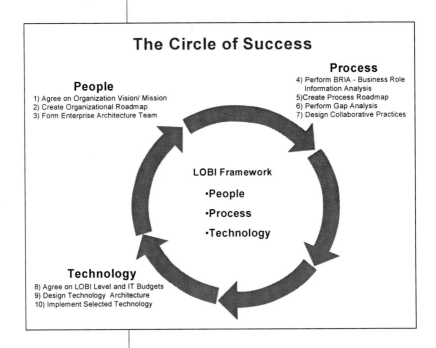

The Circle of Success

People
1) Agree on Organization Vision/ Mission
2) Create Organizational Roadmap
3) Form Enterprise Architecture Team

Process
4) Perform BRIA - Business Role Information Analysis
5) Create Process Roadmap
6) Perform Gap Analysis
7) Design Collaborative Practices

LOBI Framework

•People

•Process

•Technology

Technology
8) Agree on LOBI Level and IT Budgets
9) Design Technology Architecture
10) Implement Selected Technology

In the meantime, please take a look at the Circle of Success on the opposing page. This is a visual depiction of the ten steps in the Ladder Framework. We're now in the middle of the

People-Process-Technology model we proposed in Chapter One. Specifically, we have been discussing Steps 1, 2 and 3.

In this chapter, we have begun our discussion of People. There will be more on People in Chapter Five because this is where the key to success of the Ladder and of the company lies. If people understand and buy in to the kind of change and growth advocated by the Ladder, the company will grow and succeed. If they resist, then the company – Natural Bounty, for example – may not be able to make the changes necessary to compete in a highly competitive field. The company might not even survive.

Tom's Takeaways

Asking the Right Questions

Suppose you set a goal in your personal life to increase your income by one-and-a-half times in the next two years. One path would be to resign yourself to working longer hours. Another path might be to ask some key questions. For example, you might ask, "Can I achieve this goal by working smarter instead of harder? Can I use my experience and creativity to generate more income without knocking myself out? What are my next steps?"

Most of us have been trained in school and college to answer questions. First, information is given to us and then questions about this information are posed – always by other people. Another way of learning, however, is to get good at asking questions. Not just any questions, but key questions – the kind that produce significant answers. Intelligent questions may evoke life-changing answers – for individuals and for organizations.

The goal of the Ladder is to create intelligent businesses – and this can be accomplished by asking intelligent questions at every stage of the planning process. In the example above, an individual is working on transforming his life by asking smart questions. If every decision-maker in a business focuses on how he or she can work smarter, the entire enterprise will be transformed.

4 Down from the Mountain

By now, it should be clear that scaling the Ladder of Business Intelligence is facilitated by asking questions. Not just any questions, but significant questions. Learning how to ask the right questions creates answers that will transform a company.

In the last chapter, we identified the primary questions a company needs to ask. Where are we going? What is our vision? What is our mission? What are our core strengths, main challenges and key opportunities? The answers to these questions set the direction for the entire organization.

We then discussed the first steps necessary to bring the company vision and mission into the real world. Creating yearly objectives and goals and setting up a method for measuring progress towards those goals are some of these first steps. Creating an Enterprise Roadmap defines the business processes necessary to achieve the company goals and objectives.

In this chapter, we'll focus on these business processes. This involves asking more questions like, "What are the core processes that contribute the most to the company's bottom line? How are these processes working now? How can they be improved? What information do the owners of these processes need to know to make them work better? How can they get that information?"

These questions correspond to Numbers 4, 5 and 6 on the Circle of Success.

At Natural Bounty, the Corporate Effectiveness and Efficiency Team (CEET) is presently in the middle of asking the kind of questions listed above. We now join the team a few weeks after their first meeting portrayed in the previous chapter.

* * * * *

Sheila, Emily and Jess were already seated when Ron arrived at Sheila's office. Ron was accompanied by a dark-haired, fortyish man in a brown business suit.

Ron smiled and held out his hand to the man next to him. "Everybody, I think you know Jeffrey, our new Director of Business and IT Relationships. He'll be taking my place on this team after a few more meetings."

Emily and Sheila smiled and waved. Jess stepped forward and shook Jeffrey's hand. "Nice to have you with us," he said. He then shook Ron's hand. "I haven't had a chance to congratulate you."

Sheila raised her water bottle. "Here's to our new CIO."

As Ron and Jeffrey took their seats, Jess continued to speak to Ron. "I was away when the announcement was made. The whole thing seemed kind of sudden."

Ron shook his head. "It's actually been in the works for a while. Mike – my former boss – was never really comfortable with the Ladder concepts. He'd been considering retirement anyway, so this seemed like a good time. And Marty, his VP, decided to leave at the same time. So that left me. Randall liked the fact that I have a business background, as well as Information Technology."

"The new brand of CIO," said Emily.

"It's true," said Ron. "More and more, CIOs need to think in strategic terms, because the technology is so intertwined with business decisions. You all know this after working with the Ladder framework. In most companies I've worked for, the IT departments still focus mainly on operational, rather than strategic, tasks. We're changing that."

"Okay," said Emily, "if CIOs need to think in business terms, do CEOs and the other executives need to know more about IT? Do they need a crash course in information technology?"

"Good question," answered Ron. "In general, executives do need to know more about what IT has to offer. But with the Ladder, I'm able to show Randall the benefits of adopting the framework without his having to know all the details. And I'm able to show him the return on investment of the new software applications without his having to go back to school."

Jeffrey leaned forward. "We're talking about the CIO, but it seems like the Ladder is asking everyone in the company to think like a businessperson. Every decision maker is going to be asked what information they need to do their job better – and how they can further the company's agenda."

Ron nodded. "As the company grows, we've got to create leaders at every level. We can't escalate decisions upward any more. It just takes too long – and it overwhelms the higher-ups. Randall knows this. He knows that the managers and team leaders are the ones closest to what's really going on – so they're the ones who need to decide how to proceed."

"So our jobs will get easier because we won't have to micro-manage everything," said Sheila. "But, according the Tom and the other Ladder experts, we'll still be able to keep tabs on what's happening. We and our higher-ups can view the progress of a project or process, watch for trends and make sure that everything's aligned."

"Absolutely," said Ron. "Owners of a process or participants will have secured access to a process Web site. All the key information will be there – and it'll be updated by the system."

"I have a question," said Emily. "There are people in my department who really have no interest in thinking about the needs of the whole company. They don't think in business terms – they just want to do their job and go home. What about them? Are they going to find themselves out in the cold?"

"No, no, no," protested Ron. "That's the beauty of the Ladder framework. Going through this whole process improvement means that everybody's tasks are getting aligned with company objectives. So as long as your friends in HR do their jobs well, they will be furthering the company's business, no matter what their outlook."

"But from what I can see," said Jeffrey, "the framework is set up so that, as they operate over time, people may begin to see how their tasks make a process work better – and, maybe, even how the process fits into a greater plan. In other words, they're probably going to start thinking in strategic terms, whether they like it or not."

"Interesting," mused Emily. "A company of entrepreneurs."

"Hey, look at Southwest Air," said Sheila. "There's a company where everybody thinks that the success of the airline depends on them."

"And it does," said Jess. "This kind of involvement is the direction we want to go in. Ron is right, you don't have to have a business perspective as long as you're aligned with the company's goals. But Jeffrey is right too – this new framework is probably going to encourage a lot of people to think in strategic terms, instead of just about their job or their unit. And that can only help the company."

"So," said Emily, "the goal is to have everybody giving feedback on how to improve our business processes, how their business unit can do its job better and so on."

"Yes, indeed," answered Jess. "The process architecture that we're creating is just the beginning."

"How many processes do we have to focus on," asked Emily. "I mean there have to be hundreds in the company."

Ron stepped up to the whiteboard and began writing numbers.

"80 percent-slash-20 percent," read Emily. "Please explain."

"This is the ratio of company revenue to core processes," answered Ron. "Out of the hundreds of business processes in this company, twenty percent of them bring in eighty percent of the revenues."

"Well, it's pretty clear in a company of retail stores what a few of those core processes are," said Jess. "I mean, the process of customer shopping – there's one. Managing our supply chains – there's another."

"It's true," answered Ron, "some of them are obvious. But some of them are not, even though they're right up there in importance. So it's not just getting the processes right, it's getting the right processes right."

"And that's what we're here to do," said Sheila. "Our job as the CEET team is first to identify those core processes, then to figure out how they can be improved so that the company can reach its goals. We have to look at the gap between where each process is now and where we want it to be."

"Gap analysis," said Jess.

"But, just to clarify, we don't have to do this all alone," said Ron. "After we identify the core processes, our next job is to go to each department and help them choose an owner for the process – someone who is leading the improvement and is accountable for the result. Then we'll work with that owner and his or her team. We need their subject matter expertise to figure out how to make each process work better. These are the people who execute the process every day."

"That's one of the things I like about this Ladder process," said Emily. "Everyone involved in a process – each team member – gets to have a say."

"Yes, indeed," said Ron. "The whole point here is to get people involved. We want them to feel ownership. We want them to know that their input is valued, because it is. In a lot of places I've worked, people couldn't care less about what happens to the company – or even their business unit. They just do what their superiors tell them and try not to get in trouble. It's a fear-based culture."

"We're trying to create another kind of culture here," added Jess. "We want people involved and collaborating. And to do this, we need each team member to consider how to make their processes work better. And, yes, we want it from everyone, from the CEO to the checkout clerk in Sioux City."

* * * * *

Processes A business process can be defined as a sequence of tasks or activities that leads to a desired outcome for a specific customer. A process can be anything from billing customers to creating an educational program to designing an exhibit. In mid-sized companies, like Natural Bounty, there may be anywhere from four hundred to five hundred different processes. The Ladder framework targets the *core processes*:

the ones that fundamentally affect the performance of the company and distinguish it from the competition.

For example, at Natural Bounty markets, the *customer experience* is regarded as a core process. There are six steps to this process: customers look for various items, load them into their carts and then unload the items from the carts onto the moving belt at the checkstand. The checker adds up the items, the bagger places them in paper bags, and the customer pays the checker. This six-step sequence has a specific, desired outcome: a customer who has paid and is ready to leave the store with the groceries. (In some cases, there may be one more step: if the customer needs help, the bagger will carry the groceries out to the car.)

In many food stores, this outcome might be enough: a paid customer out the door. Natural Bounty, however, wants more than that: they want customers to come back. To ensure this outcome, the company concentrates on certain intangibles in addition to the six visible steps in the shopping experience. For example, store managers advise checkers to greet customers and ask them if they found everything they needed. The checkers and any other front line employees are also encouraged to be extra helpful and to engage in friendly conversation if the customer is open to it.

These intangibles are designed to create the ambiance of a neighborhood market – as set forth in the mission statement. So, for Natural Bounty, the *desired outcome* of the customer experience process is not just a paid customer, but a smiling, satisfied customer. This individual is likely to come back.

The friendliness and helpful concern of all front-line employees is seen as a key marker that distinguishes the Natural Bounty stores from the impersonal enormity of the supermarket chain stores and gives them their competitive edge. This is an additional reason why the customer experience process is regarded as a core process at Natural Bounty.

The customer experience is an "identity process" for Natural Bounty – that is, it distinguishes the company from other food stores, especially the large supermarket and warehouse chains (Box 1 defines process categories). An identity process is a business process for which a company is known and is essential for its survival.

Successful companies focus on and invest in their identity processes because they are among their most valuable assets. Think of Dell's customer-designed computers or amazon.com selling books over the Internet. The processes of purchasing computers or books have to be as simple and customer-friendly as possible. If they are not, customers will go elsewhere and the image and reputation of each company will suffer.

Four Process Categories

Peter Keen, in his book, *The Process Edge*, identifies four different process categories:

1. **Identity Process:** a process that distinguishes a company for itself, its customers and investors, and establishes its competitive edge.
2. **Priority Process:** a process that fundamentally affects a company's performance. It strongly influences how well Identity Processes are executed and enhances its competitiveness. (We call these "core processes")
3. **Background Process:** a process that is necessary to support, leverage, and optimize daily operations.
4. **Mandated Process:** a process that is mandatory by regulation or law

Process Improvement

The executive team at Natural Bounty has set ambitious goals for the coming year. Incorporating the recently acquired stores into the chain is at the top of the list, but the team has also set goals for improved customer experience as well as standardization in managing the supply chain for all stores.

Managing the supply chain is another of the core processes at Natural Bounty. But since the goals for the company have changed, this means that the entire process must also change in order for the company to attain its new goals. The team of

Ladder experts has advised the CEET team on the sequence of actions necessary to improve this process – and other processes.

Here are six steps involved in process improvement:

1. **Form an Enterprise Process Improvement Team**. In large companies, this team would take over the task of process improvement. The Corporate Effectiveness and Efficiency Team (CEET) team would then become a kind of steering committee for the process improvement team. However, because of the relatively small population at Natural Bounty headquarters, in this case, the existing CEET team will take on the role of the Enterprise Process Improvement Team.

2. **Create a Company Process Roadmap**. In the previous chapter, we looked at an Enterprise Roadmap. The CEET team now facilitates the creation of a *Process Roadmap* for Natural Bounty. This Process Roadmap will include input from the executives and the business units. As you can see in the illustration, a process roadmap is a list of the fundamental core processes for the company. It also depicts the order in which these processes happen and the relationships between the components of the process. For example, managing the supply chain obviously has to take place before the customer experience process.

Example for Cross Functional Process

Return Material Authorization (RMA) Process Roadmap

A cross-functional flowchart (swim lane diagram) with functions organized in rows: Customer, Company, Repair CM, Install Base, Break Fix Provider. The process flows from Start through various decision points and process steps to End.

Start → Unit Fails-calls company with a Service Request → Verifies warranty information based on Serial Number → Is the Customer covered under warranty/Service?
- No → Customer informed of his eligibility and re-routed to appropriate person
- Yes → Type of Service
  - M-B → RMA Number generated and Ship To address given to the Customer, after checking the pct family → Customer ships item to CM specified in RMA (RMA) → CM's informed about the RMA details → CM's matches the item received with the RMA details
    - Not Matching → RMA updated with the new PartNum/ Sl. Num
    - Matching → Item entered into IB-S status changed to SRCD → Repair Process at CM's end → Is there a need to replace any component?
      - Yes → Rebuild the Config → ReShips the repaired item to the Customer → Receives the repaired part
      - No → Update IB with the new Config details like new Part Num/ Sl Num/ Entitlements → **End**
  - S → Refer next sheet - Onsite Repair
- Receives the shipment notice from CM

Functions

Time / Sequence

66   Chapter 4: Down from the Mountain

3. **Choose Process Owners**. Please take note in the illustration that each core process has an owner. These places are presently blank because the owners have not yet been chosen. The CEET team must set up meetings in each department of the company, discuss the new company objectives and negotiate who will take responsibility for each core process. This process owner will be accountable for the design, performance and improvement of each process. They will report progress to the CEET team.

4. **Assess the Health of Each Core Process**. The Process Improvement Teams in each department, with the help of the CEET team, must now assess the health of each core process. Does the output of the process match the expected results? Does it meet the needs of the customer (internal or external)? Is the business activity performed efficiently? Can its performance be easily tracked?

We have created a simple set of criteria to assess the health of any particular process. The chart labeled "Process Health Criteria" on the adjoining page lists the properties of a broken process (red), a process that needs some improvement (yellow), and a process that meets or exceeds expectations (green)

Process Health Measurement Criteria

Process Health Measurement	Details
RED	•Process is ineffective and/or inefficient •Outputs do not meet customer requirements •Metrics are not identified or tracked •Performance problems exist, no cross-functional alignment
YELLOW	•Process output meets basic customer requirements •Metrics are identified, but require significant improvement •Some operational problems need resolution •Better cross-functional alignment and interlock required
GREEN	•Process meets customer needs in an efficient manner •Metrics show positive improvement trends •Process is well documented and actively managed •Effective cross-functional alignment and interlock

Prioritization of core processes is based first on the company's objectives which, in turn, are derived from the vision and mission statements. The Process Improvement Teams must decide which processes are key to fulfilling the company's mission and objectives. Second, the teams look at which processes have the greatest impact on revenue, quality, cost and customer satisfaction.

The core processes that are assessed as red will be the ones targeted for immediate attention. As an example, the process of managing the supply chain at Natural Bounty is near the top of the list. This is a core process, but the assessment is red. The process is inefficient, with poor outputs, unclear metrics and low performance. This process had problems even before the acquisition of fifty new stores and badly needs attention.

6. **Process Design: Map Core Processes "As Is", "To Be" and Perform Gap Analysis**. Improving any process requires a clear view of how the process functions at the present time – the "as is" map. The process team then needs to create a second map of how they wish the process to operate – the "to be" view. The next step is to see where the differences lie in the two process maps – the gap analysis. This analysis demonstrates clearly what parts of the process need the most attention. These may include gaps in resources, information tools, redundancies, overlaps, missing steps or missing communication.

There are certain steps that a process owner and team need to follow in order to roll out the process improvement. In process improvement workshops, the team will:

1. Define the process objectives and scope
2. Define and design the current "as is" process employing flow charts, tables, illustrations and narratives
3. Define and design the improved "to be" process employing flow charts, tables, illustrations and narratives
4. Identify all the process gaps, challenges and open issues
5. Identify key customers (the functional groups/individuals that benefit from the process outcome)
6. Identify any cross-functional collaboration necessary to the success of this process. Sometimes this involves bringing a cross-functional team to the table. For example, the forecasting process might

engage a team from Finance, Operations, Sales, Marketing and Engineering to help define a healthy process for creating an accurate forecast.

7. Decide on the success criteria for the process. Then, formulate key efficiency and effectiveness metrics to measure success. These metrics will measure whether the process is healthy – that is, whether it is achieving the objectives it was designed to achieve

8. Identify key factors for the success of this process

9. Set up a quarterly executive evaluation of the progress of core processes. The rating of progress for each process will determine the reward for the owner of the process.

A Step Back

At this point, why don't we take a step back and see where we are. A look at the Circle of Success presented in chapter 3, under the "Process" heading, shows that we're presently at Step 6 in implementing the Ladder framework

In this chapter, we've discussed some of the factors necessary to transform unhealthy processes into smooth, well-oiled operations. If a company sets new, ambitious goals, then the processes employed to achieve these goals absolutely need to be automated and running smoothly. Core processes need to move from an unhealthy red or yellow on the rating chart to an optimal performance of green.

This improvement in a company's core processes is one of the key steps in ascending the Ladder of Business Intelligence. A company will not be able to reach the higher levels of the

Ladder unless most of its core processes are rated green. Among other things, this will involve employing new business intelligence to enhance the operation of each process.

Remember the ship we described in Chapter 3 where the First Officer got the destination wrong? By definition, this made every other decision on the voyage wrong. What we've laid out in this chapter and the previous one are the ways to get the direction – and the subsequent decisions – *right*.

However, there is one more factor critical to making the voyage a successful one. This factor is *people*. Since every business is made up of people, it's critical to have everyone on board, both literally and figuratively.

If people don't understand how the changes will benefit them, they are likely to resist them. This makes Change Management a key step in implementing the Ladder framework and, not surprisingly, the topic of our next chapter.

Tom's Takeaways
The Importance of Process

In many businesses, processes are poorly understood. They are sometimes viewed as onerous, bureaucratic procedures that inhibit a more open, freewheeling style. We even heard one manager describe his company as a "process-free zone."

Yet, virtually every activity in an organization is part of some process, even in seemingly chaotic environments. Once people make this connection, they are then more open to changing and improving key processes.

Think of major league companies and you will come up with process-oriented firms. For example, VISA, Starbucks, FedEx, IBM and General Electric are masters of process. Even at Google, where the environment has been described as "controlled chaos," there are highly innovative processes for bringing new ideas to market.

Smoothly running processes will ultimately make life easier and more productive for everybody in an organization. Instead of being weighed down by onerous procedures, people will be set free to plan and innovate in a more relaxed manner.

5 People

Getting from "They" to "We"

In the last few chapters, we've talked a good deal about people working together: people formulating visions and objectives, working on improving processes, getting involved, taking responsibility for improvement. The focus may have been on improving various operations, but we must never forget who is actually doing the work. It's always about people: you, I, him, her, we, they. Ignore this and you fail, no matter how lofty your vision or desirable your goals.

Enhanced communication and collaboration *among people* is, after all, one of the key goals of the Ladder of Business Intelligence. We have discovered that improved communication needs to begin from the moment a company decides to implement the Ladder. This is because most people will resist change unless they understand how it will benefit them. To these individuals, change in the workplace is something that is imposed from the outside. When they hear "change," people tend to think "they." "'They'– the executives – are doing this to me – that is, threatening my job, my income and my comfort zone."

This chapter is about getting from "they" to "we." It's about how to manage change in such a way that people understand both the purpose of the change and the role they can play in the new order. When more and more people start saying, "*We* are accomplishing this change," that's the point when you know that the change implementation will probably be successful.

Making Life Easier

After all, one of the reasons for adopting The Ladder of Business Intelligence is to make life easier for people. It's about achieving success by working smarter instead of harder. This is, in part, accomplished by letting machines do what they do best – that is, crunch data and produce the information that people need. This leaves people with time to do what they do best – that is, employ their human intelligence. People are now free to plan, collaborate with others and, perhaps, work in a more relaxed manner.

This is life at Level 3 of the Ladder. Communication and collaboration are enhanced. Cross-functional cooperation is made easier. Meetings can be shorter and more productive because everyone present has access to the same information. With the increased visibility, executives can view progress towards their objectives and managers can fine-tune processes as they are happening. These are the benefits that reaching Level 3 can bring to people throughout the organization.

Reaching Level 3 in any organization, however, will happen only if the Change Management Team can communicate the benefits it will bring while dealing with people's resistance to change. Their job is to guide anxious people through this unfamiliar territory of change – to get them from the "as is" world to the "to be" world as smoothly as possible.

Let's join the CEET team at Natural Bounty as they grapple with their new role as the Change Management Team.

*   *   *   *   *

When Emily entered Sheila's office, Jess was standing at the whiteboard drawing little circles behind two long, curved lines. Sheila sat behind her desk, watching him. Ron moved his chair to make room for Emily.

"So, Major," said Jess, "here we have a battlefield with two opposing armies. These circles are troop concentrations of different sizes..."

Emily sat down next to Ron. "Omigod," she whispered to him, "they're doing their military thing again! I can't stand it!"

"...but they're all separated – they can't communicate. This is pre-20th century. No field radios, no cell phones, no technology at all. Messengers and flags – that's all they had. They don't have a clue what's going on."

"Yes, that's right, Lieutenant," Sheila nodded. "And neither do their commanders."

"So this side starts to advance..." Jess pointed to one of the lines on the board.

"Excuse me!" Emily broke in. "I hate to interrupt this military history class, but don't we have important things to discuss? Like why are we getting so much resistance to our Ladder implementation? Why are people acting so weird? I'm really bothered."

"Em, I know that military strategy is not your favorite topic," said Jess, "but if you'll bear with me for a few minutes, I think you'll see why this is pertinent."

"This is interesting." added Ron. "Bear with us for a little while."

Emily rolled her eyes, but nodded. "If you say so."

Jess again pointed to the curved line on the whiteboard. "So this side begins to advance. Now, what do these guys do?" He jabbed at several of the circles behind the other line. "Retreat? Advance? Stand and fight? They don't know, because they can't communicate with the officers at HQ. HQ doesn't even know because there's no aerial reconnaissance. They hardly know where their troops are, say nothing of the condition they're in. This was how battles were fought before the 20th century."

"Yeah," said Sheila, "pretty much in total ignorance."

"War is always stupid," murmured Emily.

"Hush!" said Ron.

Jess continued. "Finally, by the Second World War, they had radio communications and that changed everything. Each of these units could report back to Central Command and Command could tell them what to do. Suddenly, they knew where everybody was and what shape they were in. And not only that, Command could coordinate the air force, the navy, the artillery and so on. A battle became a coordinated exercise."

"But we're not an army," protested Emily. "We're not fighting a war."

Sheila got up and went to the whiteboard. "What Jess is saying, Em, is that each of these circles is one of our 110 stores. In order to take on the Whole Foods monster – or any competitor – we've got to be able to communicate and coordinate with all our circles. Right, Lieutenant?"

Jess nodded vigorously. "Tom – one of the Ladder experts – says that his job is to help us start out at least with field radios."

There was silence for a few moments. Sheila returned to her chair and put her elbows on the table. "Field radios" she mused. "It's funny, in less than a hundred years, we've gone from too little communication – too little data – to too much. Now the people and the technology can't even handle all the reports from the field – they come in so thick and fast. Audio, visuals... There's never enough people to gather and interpret the data."

"Are you talking about battlegrounds or businesses?" asked Ron. "Because you just described what we have to deal with in IT all the time. We've got all these stores generating data every day. The technology just can't deal with it all. In every department, we have people who do nothing but gather data; we have managers pouring over spreadsheets for hours trying to find the few bits of data they need."

"I was talking about the military," answered Sheila, "but I guess the situation is the same in our little company – our little company suddenly grown large."

"But we have this Ladder framework that's going to change things," protested Emily. "We're going to make it so they get the information they need. Why can't people see that? A lot of them are even resisting answering questions for the BRIA."

"This is one reason I'm using the military analogy, Em," answered Jess. "We may not be in a war, but it's just as imperative that we learn to communicate and coordinate. We've got to change or this company's going to go down the tubes."

"I agree," said Emily. "And I *do* see your military analogy. But every soldier in the field or in support must know that winning the battle – or just staying alive – depends on good communication and collaboration. In World War II, everyone must have welcomed the new field radios. They must all know that everything depends on everybody coordinating with everybody else. I mean, a battle is just one big, complex process, isn't it? So if all the soldiers, sailors, airmen and officers get it, why don't the folks in my HR department get it?"

Ron leaned forward. "Somehow, people are not getting that their survival is at stake. They don't understand the company's situation. The general tone is, 'Well, we've done pretty well up to now with the old ways – why change them?' They don't get that we're no longer a small company where things can get hashed out over lunch."

"Tom says that we've got to address our specific population," said Jess. "These are independent-minded people at this company. If you were into natural foods twenty years ago – even ten years ago – you were a rebel. But they made this company work and now we're asking them to change – and they're resisting."

"Okay," said Sheila, "our CEET team is the Change Management team. We have to understand why people are resisting the changes. Then we have to address each argument." She slid a pad in front of her and started writing. "First, why are people resisting?"

"Because they're stupid," fumed Emily.

"Whoa, your "E" is showing, Emily," said Jess. "V.E.C. cubed, remember? Vested Interest, Ego, and Communications at three levels. It's all about how to align people's vested interests and their egos with the message you want to communicate to them. We have to become really good communicators – and get our own egos out of the way."

"Yeah, Tom thinks that's the answer to everything," said Emily. "But I can't get through the Vs and the Es when I talk to people."

"We're 'big picture' people, said Ron. "But a lot of people don't see the big picture, and it's not because they're stupid. They just haven't been exposed to that kind of understanding. They're focused on their own work."

"Yeah, I get a lot of that," said Emily. She made her voice shrill. "'Leave me alone! I have to work with these spreadsheets. I don't have time to answer your questions.'"

"Have you tried telling them how much easier it will be when the information is right there on their display device?" asked Jess. "That if they help come up with the right questions, then we can design systems that will give them the right information just when they need it?"

"Yes, I have. The thing is, is that they like finding the data on five different spreadsheets. The reason the system is so broken is that they're all managing different Excel spreadsheets and it's all via the phone. 'What did you do, how much did you work on that? Oh, really? You have about four more hours. Okay, let's see…let me enter that piece of data here.' It's all totally fragmented. They're operating at Level 1, maybe Level 0."

"But this is what they know, Em," said Ron. "This is what they inherited from their predecessors. They feel useful when they solve problems with these tools that they've always had. And they feel threatened when we talk about new methods. They don't know how they're going to fit in or what they're going to do."

"I understand that," said Sheila. "That's how I felt when I first heard about this Ladder stuff and the team of experts. But I'm basically one of the big picture people, like the rest of you, so I got how useful this framework can be pretty quickly. Our CEO, Randall, gets it too. That's why the Ladder team is here."

"Well, maybe it's time for Randall to step up to the plate for us," said Jess. "Maybe he needs to give the other executives some incentives for implementing the framework. A few directives from on high might get people's attention."

"They may need to be financial incentives," added Ron. "Like tying the CXO's compensation to how quickly the whole program gets going."

"My boss, Jessica, in Finance gets it," said Jess. "She's with us."

"Yeah, that figures," said Ron. "In Finance, they know about process."

"But everything's a damn process – everything in the company!" exclaimed Emily. "And don't tell me to watch my 'E.'"

"That's what we need to show them," said Sheila. "We need to show them that everything they do is part of some process and that a lot the processes aren't working. We somehow need to show them that these new processes we're designing – with their input – are likely to work much more efficiently – and that their lives will get easier. The computers can do so many of these mundane tasks – finding data on the spreadsheets, for instance – that it'll free up their time. Every company that Tom and his team have worked with has shown that."

"But our people don't know that," said Ron.

"Well then, we've got to tell them," answered Sheila. "We've got to show them examples. We – all of us – have to get good at selling this product. We'll get all the help we can from Randall and whoever, but it's really up to us. We have to listen to people and we have to communicate to them all that we're not threatening their Vs and Es – we just want to get them aligned with the goals of the company... now I'm sounding just like Tom."

"We'll have more small seminars on the Ladder and the company's goals," said Jess. "We'll answer questions there, but we also need to speak to each person who is resisting. We need to tie what they do to the success of the company and then explain that the company's survival is at stake. We're trying to create a winning business model in a very competitive field."

Emily nodded. "Their lives may not be at risk, like on your battlefield, but their jobs are certainly at stake. We need to explain the big picture to them. I'll try to rein my 'E' and get good at change management communication."

"Remember to talk about the good things too," added Sheila. "Talk to them about growing their careers in a successful company. Here, Tom turned me on these people." She held up a booklet then began to read from it: "'We have developed a model to help in the change management process. Research shows that problems with the people dimension of change is the most commonly cited reason for project failure.'"

"Well, we can see that already," said Emily.

Sheila held up her hand. "The five key goals that form the basis of this model are[1]:

* Awareness of the need to change
* Desire to participate and support the change
* Knowledge of how to change – and what the change looks like
* Ability to implement the change on a day-to-day basis
* Reinforcement to keep the change in place

"I've got more copies of this booklet. I think we all need to read it. This is the 'how' of change management."

"I'll read it tonight," said Emily. "I need all the help I can get."

"We all do," said Jess. "If this Ladder implementation is going to work, as many people as possible have to understand why the company needs it and what role they can play."

*   *   *   *   *

At Natural Bounty, the CEET team is working at making people aware of the business reasons for the changes the company is undergoing. Once this understanding is gained, then the team needs to help each individual understand how he or she will fit into the new scheme of things.

We want to emphasize that the scenarios and conversations at Natural Bounty correspond to real scenarios and conversations we have had at dozens of companies over the years. For

---

1. From the ADKAR Change Management Learning Center online tutorial: www.change-management.com/tutorial-adkar-overview.htm

example, the change management techniques you are reading about in this chapter are drawn from long – and sometimes painful – experience.

At present, at Natural Bounty, many people are resisting answering questions for the Business Role Intelligence Analysis, or BRIA. This is ironic because these are the questions that will ultimately produce the information that they need to perform their roles better. These answers to key questions will make life easier and more productive for decision makers at all levels.

"Back to the Circle of Success presented in chapter 3, the BRIA is the last step (step 7) before starting to look at the information systems and technology needed for the various business units of the company. Here's a brief description of how it works."

Business Role Intelligence Analysis (BRIA)

In Chapter 3, we discussed the high-level planning process: how a company's vision is transformed into workable objectives and goals. These objectives have owners – in this case, the Vice President of each department. In addition, each of these objectives needs its own metrics so that the owner can measure its progress and health. BRIA is step 5 in the Circle of Success.

Then, in Chapter 4, we described how business processes are created and refined to achieve the company's objectives. The Business Role Intelligence Analysis, or BRIA, is the final step in creating sound processes that can be supported by a robust technology.

The BRIA process begins with the CEET team asking each decision maker to clarify his or her business role, with the help of his or her team.

What are the specific tasks of this role? What processes are involved in reaching his goals? Then, he is asked to formulate five to ten questions that he needs answered in order to perform his job better. What information does he need to appear on his display device every day, every week or every month?

In order to leverage this effort, the CEET team will prioritize the processes in a company. They will ask, "What are the core processes in this business? Which 20% of the processes bring in 80% of the revenues?"

Creating the Business Role Intelligence Analysis (BRIA)

1. Identify core processes
2. Identify key roles and decide which of these needs the BRIA
3. Define the business role name.
4. Address the key business questions (1-10) that the business role needs answered in order to be successful.
5. Identify the information required to answer those questions.
6. Identify quality data sources needed in order to generate the information to answer those questions.
7. Evaluate the time/frequency. How often does the business role need the information in order to be successful?
8. Decide how the information will be presented.
9. Decide how the information will be displayed (PDA, e-mail, application, report)

10. Identify the core processes. What are the processes that will be an input or an output for this business role?

11. Determine any additional business roles involved.

12. Determine the current level on the Ladder of this business role and determine the desired level.

The BRIA is a simple but powerful tool for assessing information technology needs. Once the BRIA has been completed for a specific set of roles within a business domain or business unit, it will become the baseline for a "Business Requirement Document." This functional specification precedes any assessment for a new information system.

Once the questions are formulated, the next step in this BRIA process is to define key metrics for each process. Each answer must be able to be broken down into measurable components. For example, if a sales manager needs figures for total sales in a particular region each month, the figures from each salesperson in that region must be retrievable within that time frame.

When the key people in Sales have completed the BRIA, technology can then be designed and chosen that will provide the answers needed by each decision maker. In the case of the sales manager, the technology will summarize the data from each salesperson and provide her with the regional figure she needs. Are sales on track to fulfilling her yearly goal, or are they lagging?

Whatever the answer, this information will allow her to make an informed, intelligent decision on how to proceed.

Earlier in the book, we emphasized the importance of asking the right questions. This is a working example. By asking the right question in the BRIA process, the sales manager will have key information at her fingertips that will enable her to make intelligent decisions and fulfill her goals. And these goals will also be aligned with the mission and objectives of the company.

The sales manager – and other decision makers – will have help in choosing the "right questions." This is often a collaborative process: she may have help from the CEET team, from her superiors and from her own sales team.

The BRIA is the last step before the process of choosing the technology systems, and it's a critical step. In order to choose the right technology, the IT team needs to know exactly what information each core business role requires. Frequency of information and accessibility are critical elements in designing the technology. For example, certain roles don't need information at the summary level (Level 3); they simply require facts and data at Levels 1 and 2. And for many roles, key information is not needed on a daily basis, but only once a week or once a month. By considering all these things, the technology can be carefully tailored to each role, and the costs minimized.

All this information is gathered in a *business requirement document* with functional specifications and an outline as guidelines for the IT team. This team will select the right system and configure the information system to support each business process and each business role in the way it was intelligently designed.

People Again

The benefits of the BRIA process may be clear to those who understand the larger picture, like the CEET team at Natural Bounty. However, it may be that many people simply won't do the BRIA – or any of the steps in the Ladder framework – unless they understand exactly how it will benefit them. If they perceive the Ladder as a threat to their day-to-day transactions and their vested interests, they will resist the change.

So what are the best ways to interest people in moving ahead? Appeal to their interest in helping the company succeed? Demonstrate how much more pleasant, interesting and creative their work can become? Offer financial incentives? Get top management more involved? Or maybe establish a sense of urgency, like Jess' military analogy? Any or all of these may appeal to certain people.

The best way we have discovered to deal with people's concerns is to make communication a two-way street. Most people do have real concerns about change and they need to know that these concerns are heard and addressed. Their work is not only their livelihood, it may also provide them with a sense of worth. A successful Change Management team will pay attention to these critical concerns as they encourage each person to move ahead.

The Intelligent Business

By enabling people to ask key questions, the BRIA brings human intelligence to bear on every role and process in the organization. "How have we performed this activity in the past? What resources do we need to improve our performance? What questions do we need answered?"

This kind of focus on core activities is key to improving performance and aligning each business role with company-wide goals. This is how an intelligent business is born. Suddenly, individuals and groups are thinking about what they actually do and considering what they need to do it even better.

This is the goal of a CEET team: to help people get to a place where they perceive the vital role they can play in the new scheme of things. The team is aiming for the realization on the part of each individual that he or she can take part in this change, in collaboration with others. This awakening of human intelligence is one of the vital steps in the creation of an intelligent business. Once it has been activated, it creates its own momentum. In our experience, people will then continue to ask important questions about their work and how it connects to the company's goals.

Looking Back

Implementing the Ladder framework is a process of ongoing education and communication. In this chapter, we have emphasized that people are ultimately what will make it work – not processes or technology or anything else. People run the company, and they are the ones who must be convinced that this new framework will benefit them and understand how it will benefit the company.

It's the job of the Change Management Team, with support from the top levels of the company (and any other allies they can get), to help each person understand the benefits, as well as his or her role in the new framework. When a growing number of people start saying "we are making the change," instead of "they are doing this to us," the change management process is likely to be successful.

We also described the BRIA process above. This formulation of intelligent questions is a critical step in the process of choosing the right software applications. The BRIA can also make people aware of their role in improving both individual and company performance. It is a key step in the creation of an intelligent business. This process is described in the next chapter.

Tom's Takeaways

"I am part of an enterprise that is striving to improve itself and I am an integral part of that process. I and we are going to become the very best we can."

This is the kind of statement that teams working together strive for. In guiding people through a change, a team can speak to each person's wish for fulfillment. Most people want to reach their full potential.

In addition, most people want the organization they work for to strive for its full potential. They want to belong to an exciting, successful, respected enterprise. They also want to know that their contribution is furthering that success. They want to feel both valuable and valued.

People need to understand that the Ladder concept brings "wholeness" to an organization. By this, we mean a wider ownership of strategies, input welcomed at all levels, and excellent communication. All these things create a sense of belonging and affirm that an individual can grow his or her career as the business grows.

"I and we are going to become the very best we can."

Tom's Takeaway #2

VEC3 – The Nine Knobs of Corporate Change Management

In the world of humans everything must be understood in terms of "vested interest" (V). Our observations are that this is almost universally true for all sets of humans in all domains. It is especially true in the corporate domain which is where we are implementing the LOBI Framework. The hypothesis is that in order to get people to change we must align the desired change to their vested interest. By V, we mean that by accomplishing our corporate change objectives, the individuals involved in the change will also attain the personal objectives that they desire. To the extent that you can make these objectives happen concurrently (or be perceived as such), you will have created a win/win situation. This is what we call the intersection of the vested interests of the human entities or for short notation, the intersection of the V's. Before you can plan how to intersect the V's, you must understand the value system of the person or persons that you want to change. We say that this value system represents a person's Ego (E). The objective is not to change this value system but to understand it. In order to intersect the V's, we must first understand the object of value that we will need to put into the intersection so we will both see our collaboration as mutually beneficial. Unless this occurs, effective change management will be impossible. Finally, we must use various communication (C) techniques to explain why an intersection of the V's will result in a win/win for all involved. This triplet, VEC, represents vested interest, ego and communication.

In a corporation, there are three major groups of people for whom we must learn to master the VEC concepts. The first group consists of the executives of the corporation who define the transformation vision and "allocate the resources" to be used in the transformation. The second group consists of middle management (MM) who "lead and deploy" the resources that have been allocated. Finally, the third group consists of the first line managers and their employees who actually "perform the transformation". Since we are dealing with three dimensions of people, the short form notation for referring to all three groups is VEC cubed (VEC3). The VEC3 model asserts that there are nine knobs to manage change involving people in a corporation at all times. A change leader must be aware of the state of all nine knobs. Either the change leader or a member of the change team must be accountable for making sure that the V intersections are occurring for all three groups concurrently. In order for a major change management initiative to be successful, the Vs of all three groups must intersect. The challenge for the change management team is how to align all the Vs of all three groups in a timely manner? This book shows how the LOBI framework can achieve this alignment by following the ten steps of the circle of success.

As the LOBI framework leads you through the circle of success, the alignment process requires that you focus on each of the three groups, separately, as you traverse the circle. All the key executives must be aligned before you complete step 3 on the circle, all of the key middle managers must be aligned before you complete step 7, and all of your implementation managers and their employees should be aligned when you pursue step 8. The initiation of step 8 sets in motion the largest financial investment in the technological transformation of a business. Hence, the technological transformation should not be undertaken until all three groups involved or impacted by the transformation have been brought into alignment. Many technology investments have been wasted or used ineffectively, since they were initiated without first ensuring that the nine knobs were positioned to align the three groups, yet step 8 was launched anyway. This should not be done.

Once the executive team has set the vision and the objectives of the business transformation, it is usually the middle management group that is most difficult to get on board. This difficulty is directly proportional to the number of layers in middle management. Our experience has taught us that middle management who are not aligned can utilize many techniques to hinder and ultimately moth-ball any business transformation that they have been asked to implement. The change management leader must first understand the culture of the company and then build partnerships with the key middle management leaders that "get it" using the VEC3 concepts. During the middle management alignment process there will be many "Significant Emotional Events" (SEEs). A "SEE" is normally represented as a "crisis situation" by those resisting change. Just remember that all "crisis situations" offer an opportunity for significant improvement if the change management leaders remain objective and patient.

Middle management can resist change through three classical techniques. The first technique is to "shoot" the change management leader. The resisting managers accomplish their goal by discrediting the change management leader, hoping that the executive team will loose faith in them and replace them or they will quit. The second technique utilizes what we call the "atomic unit of complexity". The resisting managers create a very complex business process that only they and their supporters understand

and ensure the business executives if this process is changed the business will fail. Unless the change management team can create a way to break through this atomic unit to understand the real risk, the middle management group resisting change will usually prevail. The final technique is passive resistance. Middle management will overtly agree to the business transformation but behind the scenes they will passively resist it. In a very large organization, all three techniques can be utilized concurrently.

Steps 4 through 7 of the circle of success allow the change management leader to bring about VEC3 alignment and minimize the impact of the three techniques on the business transformation. The Es of the middle management group can be managed by selecting strong middle management leaders as part of the change team who are committed to the business transformation.

The more successful change management efforts enlist managers from the middle management pool who believe in the business transformation and utilize them to "sell" the vision to their peers. In addition, the selected mangers should participate in a 2-3 day training session on how to manage the intersection of the Vs for the middle management group.

The last three knobs are the VEC3 knobs associated with the managers responsible for the implementation of the business and technology transformation. This is the action management group and they have to be aligned for action. This group delivers the results. Hence, this is where team training has its biggest payoff before the implementation starts. Meyers–Briggs or similar training will prove to be very useful before you begin steps 8 through 10 of the circle of success. Roles, responsibilities and bonus plans should be put in place to align the Vs of this group before implementation begins. We strongly recommend that these alignment meetings be facilitated by outside consultants. This guarantees more objectivity as the alignment strategy and goals are defined.

In summary, we have briefly described the people dynamics involved in a major business transformation. There are three people dimensions, represented by VEC3, that give change management leaders nine knobs through which they can effect business transformations. The power of using this concise mental model of your business environment is that it keeps you, the change management leader, very focused during the transformation. Obviously, a significant business transformation is very challenging and should only be undertaken if the executive team is clear on its goals, is committed to making it happen, and understand the challenges they will face. Finally, they must believe in the value of their vision.

Good luck on your nine-knob alignment voyage.

6 Implementing Technology

Chapters 3, 4 and 5 dealt with the best ways to focus human intelligence on improving business activities and managing change. These involved People and Processes. In this chapter, we will describe the implementation of the third part of our Ladder trio: Information Technology. On the Circle of Success, presented in chapter 3, this corresponds to Steps 8, 9 and 10.

In Chapter 2, we described the Ladder as a "recipe for success." The Ladder framework enables people to transform their firm into an extraordinary company.

These extraordinary results start when people begin to focus their core talents on how they manage the people, processes and technology in their business. This focus begins with the building of teams to effect the necessary changes: the high-level Executive Team that formulates the company vision, mission and objectives, the Enterprise Process Improvement Team, and the Corporate Effectiveness and Efficiency Team (CEET). (At Natural Bounty, the CEET team is also the Process Improvement Team. Larger companies might have two separate teams.)

The CEET team helped to create metrics for measuring progress towards the company objectives. They also defined the core processes in the company and began focusing on how to improve and streamline these processes. They chose owners for these core processes and, last, but not least, they worked at change management – helping people through from the "as is" to the "to be" world (Chapter 5).

A Critical Point

We are now at a critical point in our journey up the Ladder. This is the point at which human intelligence is encoded into technological information (machine intelligence). It has been our experience that most businesses are not skilled at making this connection. In most technology implementations, there is very little connection between the multimillion-dollar acquisition of IT systems and applications and the real needs of the business.

In these cases, the people making the decisions about the design and purchase of the new applications are not adept at linking these elements together. They often do not understand the impact of the new system on the business operations and the existing IT architecture.

The power of the Ladder framework is that it enables the right people to make the right connection to the business needs and to the existing IT infrastructure. These experts – the IT architects and analysts – select, analyze, design and implement new tools that will support both.

How does this happen? How do all the ingredients we discussed in Chapter 3, 4 and 5 get baked into the technology? It happens through a very detailed management of the life cycle of the IT system. This starts with process prioritizing and improvement, finding owners for the core processes and the Business Role Intelligence Analysis (BRIA). This information is then distilled into documents that describe in increasingly specific terms the exact requirements for the new information system. The progression is from a Business Requirement document to a Business Specification document to an IT Architecture document and a Configuration document.

The system is then unit tested, module by module. If this is successful, the next step is Integration testing. This testing ascertains that the end-to-end process designs are indeed translated into the technology. During Integration testing, the end user confirms whether the IT system is successful at answering his or her questions as formulated in the BRIA.

At this point, the IT architects and IT analyst confirm that the new, selected system is indeed aligned and integrated with the other systems. They also recommend the vendor – in-house or external – who will actually build the system. The requirements for the vendor to fulfill are summarized in a Request for Proposal (RFP) document. In this final process of selecting the vendor, decisions regarding the "as is" architecture, to the "to be" architecture, the desired Ladder level and the budget all come into play. Once these decisions have been made, the vendor can be selected and the system implemented.

A successful implementation means that the new information system will be integrated with the needs of each business user, with the existing IT system <u>and</u> with the direction of the company as a whole.

This is the power of the Ladder framework. The human intelligence that formulated all the improvements described in Chapters 3, 4 and 5 now has a powerful ally. The new tools and applications will support the needs of each business role, enabling intelligent, rapid decisions.

This is a good time to remember that the Ladder is composed of a *sequence* of steps. Each of the steps on the Circle of Success needs to be fully implemented before going on the next. To disregard this may prevent the Ladder from becoming an integral part of the framework of a business – and performance, quality, innovation and revenue may be impacted as a result.

To illustrate just how the final steps of the Circle are accomplished, let's listen to Ron, the new CIO at Natural Bounty, explain the process to the CEET team.

* * * * *

Natural Bounty

"So, Ron," asked Emily, "when is D-day?"

Ron nodded. "We bring the new system up in exactly two weeks."

"And how is it going?"

"It's going as well as can be expected in a company with a few dozen different legacy systems – we're not counting the stores here, just us at HQ. From the time this company was started thirty years ago, each department – sometimes each individual – developed its own business intelligence and tools. Then you've got patches on top of patches of customized tools and systems. When we did our "as-is" assessment of the technology systems and applications here, we had to add a month to our schedule."

"Because of the complexity of the different systems," asked Sheila.

"Partly because of the systems and partly because of the complexity of people and politics," answered Ron. "As we have seen, it's often people that are the biggest stumbling block. My IT team and I were prepared for the complexity of the systems, but we had to bring in Tom and his Ladder team to advise us on how to deal with the people."

"Seems like there were particular problems from Marketing," said Jess. "They fought us all the way on our process improvement, the BRIA..."

"Marketing," moaned Ron. "More than any other department, they've developed their own proprietary information system. Only a few people know how to work it."

"A *proprietary* information system?" asked Emily.

Ron shook his head. "I've seen it in a number of companies. One power tower selects a type of system and application and installs it separately from the rest of the technology systems. They live in a non-integrated world of their own making and they fight moving into the integrated world. They say that their system works great and, according to them, if they have to give it up they won't be able to do their job – and the company will suffer.

Role- Process-Technology- Evolution

Improve Technology and Business Processes

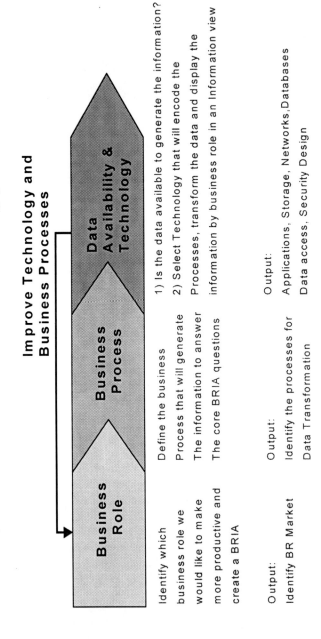

Business Role

Identify which business role we would like to make more productive and create a BRIA

Output:
Identify BR Market

Business Process

Define the business Process that will generate The information to answer The core BRIA questions

Output:
Identify the processes for Data Transformation

Data Availability & Technology

1) Is the data available to generate the information?
2) Select Technology that will encode the Processes, transform the data and display the information by business role in an Information view

Output:
Applications, Storage, Networks,Databases Data access, Security Design

Chapter 6: Implementing Technology

"So I went to Randall and said, 'Look, you've got to talk to these guys.' And he said, 'I already have and what if they're right? What if they can't do their job without their special information system and it brings down the company?' They had him scared. I had to set up a meeting with Tom, Randall and me to reassure him."

"But I'm curious about how you dealt with this," said Sheila. "I mean they seem to be on board now in Marketing, even after all the kicking and screaming."

"What Tom advised," said Ron, "was not to fight them head-on, but simply to proceed with the as-is assessment. This includes an assessment of the cost of maintaining the current systems. My team and I have to understand the maintenance costs, depreciation, a yearly maintenance expense and a yearly sustaining engineering expense. All this comes to what I call 'total cost of ownership.'"

"So, you did an assessment of the as-is tech architecture – all these different systems," said Sheila. "And you determined the cost of the operating the present system. What was next?"

"That assessment is Number 8 on the Circle," said Ron. "Step number 9 was to target the operational level we're shooting for – what level of business intelligence do we want to get to? This was one of the things we figured out in Steps 1 through 7. In our case, we're aiming for Level 4 on the Ladder. This is critical because the level where you want to operate determines the type of systems you choose and how you integrate it with the existing architecture. And this is a big factor in the cost of the technology.

"So once we decided on our target level, we could estimate the cost and work with Randall and with Gail at Finance on a budget and a time frame. Needless to say, we had to develop an affordable budget."

"But how do you estimate all the advantages of reaching Level 3 and then, Level 4?" asked Sheila. "I mean, we really need this new system. We can't continue with the old ones. And we have to tie in the stores too."

"Yes," said Ron, "we are operating from a position of desperation, rather than aspiration. Because of this emergency situation, we've been promised an expanded budget if we need it."

"I'm beginning to see what you've been doing for the last eleven months," said Emily. "And we're not even to step number 10."

Ron got up and went to the whiteboard. There, he wrote "Reference Architecture."

"Reference architecture is another term for the as-is and to-be worlds," he said. "The as-is architecture refers to all our systems, applications and infrastructure. After we know this, then we can begin to build a new reference architecture based on our new goals – and then define the gaps between the two reference architectures. We've got to agree on the to-be technology that will satisfy the key business role and the level they would like to achieve.

"We're back to gap analysis," smiled Jess.

"Yes," said Ron, "and it's pretty critical here in step 10 because we have to come up with a correction plan for each gap. The gap analysis is essentially what creates the rollout and

implementation plan for the new technology."
Then, we can do an estimated total cost of
ownership for the new system and compare it
with the old."

"Is this where you got the Marketing people?"
asked Sheila. "Were you able to demonstrate
that the new Intelligence system would work
better and cheaper than their private system?"

"Essentially, yes," said Ron. "They still took a
while to come around. Randall leaned on them,
some of the other CXOs leaned on them...."

"Don't you love company politics?" asked Emily.

Jess spoke to Ron. "So the technology may be
ready in two weeks, but are we ready? I've been
seeing a lot of anxious people around here
recently."

Ron sat down and shook his head. "A certain
amount of anxiety seems to be unavoidable.
Remember, I've told people that the processes
are going to be different and their jobs are going
to be different. We've all done our best to
evangelize about the benefits of the new system
– key information at your fingertips, no more
cutting and pasting and all that, but there's still a
lot of anxiety. Some are worried about being laid
off because they know this new system is going
to be more efficient. I've tried to show everybody
what the new technology is going to look like.
We've done unit testing, integration testing and
user acceptance scenario pilots."

"The pilots were helpful," said Emily. "I think it
was the fourth pilot where we got to practice and
give feedback."

"That was the end user pilot," said Ron. "First, we tested the customizations, how the system works with end-to-end processes and the load of performance testing – how well the system handles a real-world load. Then finally, we get to the fourth conference room pilot, which is kind of a pre-user acceptance test. 'So, okay, we've done all this stuff, we designed it, tested it. Now tell me, guys, is it ready to go?'"

"And if it isn't?" asked Sheila. "What do we do if you bring the system up in two weeks and it doesn't work the way it's supposed to?"

Ron spread out his hands. "That would be a case where 'CIO' stands for 'Career Is Over.' First we do our best to make it work. If we can't, we go back to the old system soon enough so that we haven't lost transactions – and customers."

"This happens?" said Emily, wide-eyed.

"This happens," said Ron. "I don't think it's going to happen here because we've finally got everybody on board. Most people are motivated to make it work. Systems are much more likely to fail when people aren't aligned behind the new technology. But there's still going to be a steep learning curve once we bring it up."

* * * * *

Saving Money

Even though Natural Bounty desperately needs a new information system, cost is still very much a factor – as it would be in any organization. The Ladder keeps technology costs down in two distinct ways.

First, the specificity of the questions chosen by each business role in the BRIA process enables the technology to be carefully matched to the needs of each key process and key business role. This matching means that spending on technology is minimized. For example, certain functions, like order management, operate at Levels 1 and 2; these functions need only facts and data. Supervisors in this department will need information at the summary level – Level 3 – but there is no need to spend money to provide this capability at the lower levels.

Second, the Business Requirement documents specify the information retrieval time specific to each business role. How frequently the data needs to be updated depends on how critical are the business role and the business process. Less critical functions may need to be updated less frequently, thus saving money on server time, backup and processing time.

In other words, the Ladder framework allows the business processes and the intelligence of the organization to be baked into the information system. Focusing on the specific information needs of each business role keeps costs down. This is how the Intelligent Business chooses the right configuration and design of technology.

Technology Evolution Using LOBI

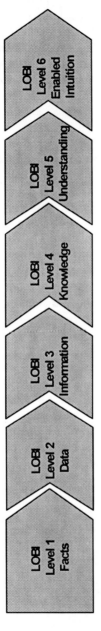

LOBI Level 1 Facts	LOBI Level 2 Data	LOBI Level 3 Information	LOBI Level 4 Knowledge	LOBI Level 5 Understanding	LOBI Level 6 Enabled Intuition
Networks	Security Systems	BI, OLAP	Data Mining	Strategic	Neural Networks
Internet connectivity	Advanced Networks	BAM, BPM	Knowledge Management	Collaborative tools	Brain Augmentation
PBX	Central Storage	BR Info Display	Expert Systems	shareware	Pattern Recognition
email, WANS	Servers farms	Graphics	Collaboration tools	Collaborative Decisions	Technologies
Servers	Databases	Metrics	Knowledge sharing and	Adaptive self Corrective systems	
Basic Security	Integrated Applications	Dashboards Reporting	Search engines		
Direct Attach	Mobility devices		Artificial Intelligence		
Storage	Process Management				
Desktop	Tools and monitoring				
Computers	Content Management				
Spreadsheets	Data Warehouse				
	Formatted Reporting				

Ongoing Process Management

In Chapters 3, 4 and 5, we discussed the creation of a process architecture, particularly for the core processes of an enterprise. The process owners, with help from the CEET and executive sponsors, design processes that fit the company's strategies and needs for the foreseeable future. But process management is an ongoing thing: organizations change, markets change and economic climates change. This means that processes must be monitored like any other valuable asset, like revenue or number of customers. We recommend a review and improvement of core processes at least once or twice a year.

This kind of process improvement is enabled when the new technology is introduced. Decision makers now have the visibility they need into the health of a process and how well it is serving its customers' needs. If there are challenges, they are able to see clearly how to address them and assign responsibility for improvement.

For example, at Natural Bounty, creating a pleasant and satisfying shopping experience for customers is a core process. They call it the "Customer Experience process." Maintaining and managing the feedback about this Customer Experience process will be an ongoing thing. This includes obtaining feedback from key executers of the process as well as from the customers themselves. There will be at least quarterly reviews of the health of this process and of customer satisfaction.

Process Health Measurement Criteria

Process Health Measurement	Details
RED	•Process is ineffective and/or inefficient •Outputs do not meet customer requirements •Metrics are not identified or tracked •Performance problems exist, no cross-functional alignment
YELLOW	•Process output meets basic customer requirements •Metrics are identified, but require significant improvement •Some operational problems need resolution •Better cross-functional alignment and interlock required
GREEN	•Process meets customer needs in an efficient manner •Metrics show positive improvement trends •Process is well documented and actively managed •Effective cross-functional alignment and interlock

Recapping

In this chapter, we've presented the final step in the implementation of the Ladder framework: adding the new information system. Information technology and information systems need to be designed and implemented so that business strategy is baked into their design. This strategy is translated into business roles and business processes. Then, in order for these processes to run smoothly, the design has to specify exactly what information each role needs, as well as the frequency with which this information needs to be delivered.

In addition, the design needs to incorporate an open architecture and make the processes scaleable and modular enough that continuous improvement is possible over time. Successful implementation of these software applications will bring an organization up to Level 3. With the proper design described above, further ascent to the upper levels of the Ladder is now possible.

In the next chapter, we'll take a look at these upper levels. We'll also discuss the environment of a company operating at Levels 3, 4, 5 and 6. What does life look like at these levels? What is now possible?

Tom's Takeaways
Level 2 on the Internet

Suppose you want to know how many startup companies there were in 2005 in the U.S. You go to Google and key in certain words: "Number U.S. startup companies 2005" and you get 3,590,000 responses. This is life at Level 2: more data than you could possibly want, but you are expected to do the filtering. The technology is not yet able to deal with the phrase, "how many." It can only present you with articles in which the key words figure prominently. Somewhere in these 3,590,000 articles on startup companies are the figures you want, but you will have to search for them.

At some point, Google and other search engines will reach Level 3. You will be able to ask a question in normal English and get an answer at the Information level. Science fiction writers have known for decades that this is where we're heading. For example, in the 1960s Star Trek series, when Captain Kirk asks a question of the ship's computer, he gets a real answer in a pleasant female voice.

Nevertheless, even in the early 21st century, it's possible to work at the Information level. Employing technology in an intelligent manner, according to the Ladder framework, will put your company ahead of 90% of the competition. A business functioning at Levels 3 and up will always have a big competitive edge over businesses at Levels 1 and 2.

7 A New Way of Doing Business

There is at least one point in the history of any company when you have to change dramatically to rise to the next performance level. Miss the moment and you start to decline.
Andrew S. Grove[2],
Chairman, Intel Corporation

With the implementation of the information technology system, the Ladder framework is now in place. Following the ten steps of the Circle of Success brings a business to Intelligence Level 3. In this chapter, we'll take a look at what we've created – and how we got there. Our goal is always to create and sustain an intelligent business – one that is able to deliver high quality products to its customers, stay ahead of its competitors, and make life easier and more productive for its managers.

Here's another look at the qualities of an Intelligent Business.

The Intelligent Business:

*   Employs human intelligence at its fullest capacity
*   Employs business intelligence optimally

2. Andrew S. Grove, "How (and Why) to Run a Meeting," Fortune 11, July 1983, 132.

- Uses superior information to enable effective decision making, communication and robust cross functional collaboration
- Uses the above three capabilities to create seamless business processes and a robust infrastructure
- Encourages innovation at every level of the organization
- Employs all of the above capabilities to operate successfully in all business environments
- Is always proactive, never complacent.

Building Bridges

Chapters 3, 4, 5 and 6 dealt with the processes involved in creating an intelligent business. These processes can be viewed as a bridge from the "as is" world in an organization to the "to be" world. With that in mind, let's take a brief view of different kinds of bridges.

A beautiful suspension bridge, like the Golden Gate Bridge could be a source of inspiration to a student of structural engineering. However, just studying exactly how the bridge was built in the 1930s is not sufficient. The student needs to also study the latest building techniques, materials science, mathematics and computer modeling to build the bridges of tomorrow. Only by mastering these disciplines will this future engineer ensure that his bridges will stand and endure.

Similarly, it can be inspiring to observe successful companies and view their unique qualities. However, while such a study may yield some useful pointers, caveats and guidelines, it will probably not tell you exactly how your company can be successful. This is because each world class business has arrived at the top by a different route. Imitating these routes is made even more difficult because these companies achieved major league status in different times and different business environments.

By contrast, the Ladder of Business Intelligence can be viewed as a direct route to success for businesses in the 21st century – a bridge from the "as is" world to the "to be" world. Building a bridge to tomorrow, however, requires a thorough mastery of each step of the Ladder process. There are no shortcuts – no quick technological fixes or simple management techniques – that will shorten this route.

Quick fixes may focus on one or more actions – say, improving a firm's business processes or information retrieval. But what good does it do to strengthen your company's skills if it has no coherent vision or clear objectives. Without knowledge of your direction, you will simply get to the wrong place faster. This is why we emphasize mastery of each step on the Ladder in the proper sequence.

The previous chapters have outlined the sequence of actions necessary to create an intelligent business. This has been a progression from Vision to Mission to Objectives to Metrics to Processes, People and, finally, to Information Technology.

As each step on the Ladder is mastered and instilled into the DNA of a business, the entire company begins to be transformed. In Chapter 1, we encouraged you to aim high – not to settle for incremental change or a quick fix, but, rather, deep change at the organizational level. Let's take a look at what this transformation looks like by comparing businesses at Levels 1 and 2 with intelligent businesses functioning at the higher levels of the Ladder.

- **Vision and mission**: Many lower-level businesses have no clear, realistic vision of where they want to go. Or, perhaps, a company at Level 1 or 2 may actually know where it wants to go, but be unable to marshal the necessary resources to get there.

At Levels 3, 4 and 5 on the Ladder, a business has defined its vision, mission and objectives and mapped out the steps necessary to accomplish them.

- **Alignment, Collaboration**: At Level 1, business roles (BRs) work as individuals; at Level 2, BRs work in silos within a business unit. There is little alignment of purpose or cross-functional collaboration.

At the upper levels of the Ladder, business roles are aligned across the organization to work for common objectives. There is robust cross-functional collaboration and alignment with customer needs.

- **Use of Information**: Data is not integrated at Level 1. At Level 2, transactional data is integrated and retrievable, but must be evaluated carefully to answer a business question. The cycle time to information (CTI) is lengthy.

At Level 3, the information system integrates data into information that answers key business questions (as formulated in the BRIA process). The CTI is short.

- **Quality of Decisions**: The quality of business decisions is limited at Levels 1 and 2. This is due to poor alignment with company vision and objectives, a slow cycle time to information, imperfect quality of information and limited collaboration in decision making.

At the upper levels of the Ladder, the information system provides decision makers with answers to their key business questions. Because all business roles are aligned with the company's vision and objectives and have access to high quality information, the roles are able to collaborate in making key decisions. This makes for rapid and high quality decisions.

- **Waste**: Levels 1 and 2: Without proper alignment of purpose, skillful use of technology and strong collaboration, most tasks consume a great deal of time, effort and money. For example, pouring over spreadsheets to gather key information from bits of data is a monumental time-waster. Meetings are often spent exchanging information instead discussing strategic planning. Human intelligence that could be focused on improving business activities, is instead involved in trying to bring order out of chaos.

A business functioning at Levels 3, 4 and 5 uses all its resources at their fullest capacity. People, Product and Technology are aligned and employed in an intelligent manner.

- **Business results**: Because of the many difficulties described above, businesses at Levels 1 and 2 may have trouble improving the quality of their products and services, keeping up with customer demands and bringing innovative concepts to market.

With company-wide alignment, quality information and robust collaboration, upper-level companies perform in a different league. They remain in touch with – or anticipate – customer needs, improve the quality of their services and bring innovative products to market in record time.

Charts 1, 2 and 3 on the adjoining pages present a detailed view of businesses functioning at different levels of the Ladder. These charts demonstrate the evolution of business roles, processes and technology as a business progresses up the Ladder.

In the real world, these comparisons between lower level and upper level businesses are not intellectual projections, but observations from experience. We have seen all these benefits in companies that have adopted the Ladder framework. When people begin to focus their intelligence on improvement, profound changes can occur.

Consider that this intelligence may have been focused mainly on how to make things work in chaotic environments. In organizations where processes operate inefficiently or ineffectively, people need to work extra hard just to keep things going. In these environments, people move data around and make decisions with guesswork while trying to restore order and please their managers. These are the kind of organizations that produced the sayings below.

Business Role Evolution using LOBI

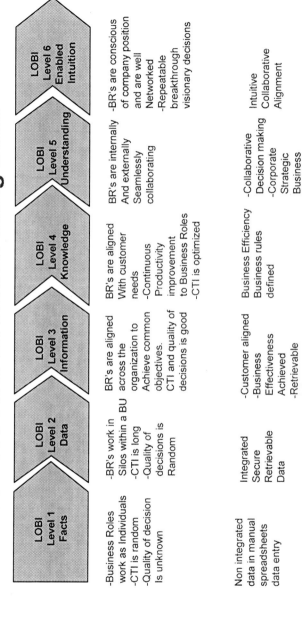

LOBI Level 1 Facts	LOBI Level 2 Data	LOBI Level 3 Information	LOBI Level 4 Knowledge	LOBI Level 5 Understanding	LOBI Level 6 Enabled Intuition
-Business Roles work as Individuals -CTI is random -Quality of decision Is unknown	-BR's work in Silos within a BU -CTI is long -Quality of decisions is Random	BR's are aligned across the organization to Achieve common objectives. CTI and quality of decisions is good	BR's are aligned With customer needs -Continuous Productivity improvement to Business Roles -CTI is optimized	BR's are internally And externally Seamlessly collaborating	-BR's are conscious of company position and are well Networked -Repeatable breakthrough visionary decisions
Non integrated data in manual spreadsheets data entry	Integrated Secure Retrievable Data	-Customer aligned -Business Effectiveness Achieved -Retrievable information views	Business Efficiency Business rules defined	-Collaborative Decision making -Corporate Strategic Business Alignment	Intuitive Collaborative Alignment

Process Evolution Using LOBI

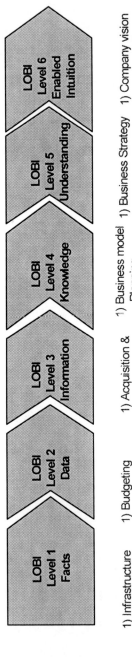

LOBI Level 1 Facts	LOBI Level 2 Data	LOBI Level 3 Information	LOBI Level 4 Knowledge	LOBI Level 5 Understanding	LOBI Level 6 Enabled Intuition
1) Infrastructure	1) Budgeting	1) Acquisition & Investment	1) Business model Planning	1) Business Strategy	1) Company vision
2) Facilities Mgmt	2) Purchasing	2) PMO	2) Software and Hardware Development LCM	2) Collaboration Process, internal and External	2) Product Strategy
3) Networks Mgmt	3) Order Fulfillment	3) Revenue Management	3) Pricing	3) Product and Service innovation	3) Business Model Simulation
4) Security Mgmt	4) Supply Chain	4) Marketing	4) Sales Compensation		4) Intuitive Innovation
	5) Data Center Mgmt		5) Forecasting		

Technology Evolution Using LOBI

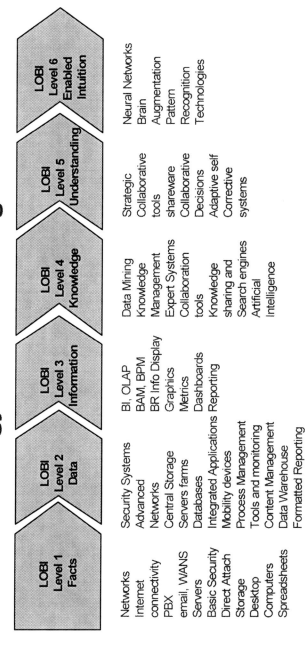

LOBI Level 1 Facts	LOBI Level 2 Data	LOBI Level 3 Information	LOBI Level 4 Knowledge	LOBI Level 5 Understanding	LOBI Level 6 Enabled Intuition
Networks	Security Systems	BI, OLAP	Data Mining	Strategic	Neural Networks
Internet connectivity	Advanced Networks	BAM, BPM	Knowledge Management	Collaborative tools	Brain Augmentation
PBX	Central Storage	BR Info Display	Expert Systems	shareware	Pattern Recognition
email, WANS	Servers farms	Graphics	Collaboration	Collaborative	Technologies
Servers	Databases	Metrics	tools	Decisions	
Basic Security	Integrated Applications	Dashboards Reporting	Knowledge sharing and	Adaptive self Corrective	
Direct Attach	Mobility devices		Search engines	systems	
Storage	Process Management		Artificial		
Desktop	Tools and monitoring		Intelligence		
Computers	Content Management				
Spreadsheets	Data Warehouse				
	Formatted Reporting				

Life at Level 1

Another deadline, another miracle.

It's not procrastination – it's the incredible Just-in-Time Workload Management System!

Any simple problem can be made insoluble if enough meetings are held to discuss it.

We, the unwilling led by the unknowing are doing the impossible for the ungrateful.

On a more positive note, here's a famous saying revised to fit the Ladder framework:

God grant me the serenity to accept the things I cannot change, the courage to change the things I can, and the equipment, training, and staff to make it all happen.

Operating Intelligently

In a business functioning at the upper levels of the Ladder, all the effort and intelligence required just to keep things going is instead focused on improving the way the business operates. A new paradigm has been created in which the awareness and intelligence brought by the Ladder are ingrained in the DNA of the business. When people operate in a more collaborative environment where processes are operating smoothly, their intelligence is released to plan, strategize and collaborate.

As we discussed in Chapter 6, the final ingredient in this recipe is the information technology. Once people have set up the framework and asked the key questions, choosing the right technology can leverage the entire operation. By providing people with the critical information they need, this new business intelligence frees them to use their intellects instead of constantly reacting to chaotic environments.

So, one reason that amazing things can happen when you work with the Ladder is that, in the course of this work, human intelligence is activated and focused on improving business activities. People get good at asking key questions and this skill enables them to become analysts and catalysts for change. New leaders are created at every level of the organization.

In addition, because these new capabilities are encouraged and rewarded, they will continue once the new framework is in operation. *It is this engagement of the human mind, coupled with carefully chosen information technology that creates the bridge to the higher levels.*

Employing information intelligently defines Level 3 on the Ladder. But Level 3 is also a plateau from which the higher levels of intelligence may be reached. We'll discuss Levels 4, 5 and 6 later in the chapter.

Right now, however, let's revisit our friends at Natural Bounty. The new information system has been up and running for a month and the CEET team is discussing the changes they're experiencing.

* * * * *

"So, Emily," said Ron, "the lowly have risen. HR is the proud owner of one of the core processes we're working on."

Emily smiled. "HR hasn't gotten any respect around here for a long time. But the reason that an HR process made the core process list is that Sheila and her team realized that having experienced employees in the stores is a key part of the customer experience."

Sheila nodded. "Shoppers like familiar faces – people who recognize them and can help them. It's part of the corner grocery feeling that we're trying to create. What's more, experienced employees know what's needed – and they know when things are out of whack. So, in this food retail business, where high turnover is taken for granted, we're trying to retain good employees."

"Yes," said Emily, "and, of course, this can also save us the cost of hiring and training. But another thing I have in the back of my mind is Level 5 on the Ladder – you know, this place that Tom talks about where everybody in the company understands what's going on, kind of intuitively. It seems to me that if we can get there, we'll have instant alignment – people knowing what to do before they're asked. It'll be high-level collaborating with people who have a real knowledge of how our operations work."

"And what you're saying, Em," said Jeffrey, "is that this level of understanding can best be reached by people who have been with the company for a while."

"Exactly," answered Emily. "This is one reason why we've got this program going to retain the best people – not just in the stores, but here at HQ too."

"How about you, Sheila?" asked Jess, "How is this new system working with your Customer Experience process?"

Sheila shook her head and smiled. "It's like night and day. Let me give you an example. It used to be that each store had a different way of dealing with customer complaints and suggestions. Some of these approaches worked okay, others didn't work at all. It was not only totally inefficient, it also meant we were losing customers. A real mess."

"So, part of our new Customer Experience process covers the best ways to deal with customer issues and problems. You know, gathering customer feedback, dealing with the feedback, creating improvements to the process...."

"At this point, most our stores have adopted these new procedures and already we're seeing improvements. We've been interviewing customers and hearing that they feel we're really listening to them – which we are."

Jess nodded. "Can you give us a capsule version of how you and your team are getting the store managers to adopt the new Customer Experience process?"

"Sure," said Sheila. "First, we mapped out the whole process, starting with where we want to get to, then, all the different steps in the process that will get us there. We set up a Web site on our Intranet and we laid out what we need from all our store managers. I sent out a long email to each manager explaining how improving customer experience will benefit every store. Don, our COO, posted a letter on our Web site saying how important this program is and tying performance to compensation. You know, we essentially have to sell this program to each store manager – show what's in it for each of them."

"But," said Ron, "you no longer have to do this one store at a time."

"No, we don't, thank heavens," answered Sheila. "My team and I do have to answer questions and complaints, but a lot of these are similar, so we put up a FAQs page on the site. I still have to talk to a few store managers and send out emails, but nothing like before. My team and I have a staff meeting every week to monitor progress – and I meet every month with Don and his executive staff."

"All the information is stored in a process repository, including process flows, guidelines, metrics, and ideas for improvement. My process health dashboard with the green, yellow, red lights shows me how healthy the process is – and what areas need improvements from the customer perspective."

Emily nodded. "All this, so a customer in Twin Falls can find the right brand of organic yogurt – and maybe have a few laughs with the staff."

Sheila smiled. "One of the goals of the Customer Experience process is to have people leave the store feeling better than when they came in. If we can accomplish this at a high percentage, people will come back. All this effort is keep people coming back to the stores – and they will, if they find what they want and enjoy themselves in the process – and know that their feedback is being listened to."

Ron leaned forward. "That pre-Ladder scenario that Sheila talked about where each store had its own way of doing things – that kind of chaos was repeated over and over, with our stores and here at HQ. Most of our processes just weren't working very well. You all know how difficult it was – how it still is in some areas. We're still in transition, but the transition is working."

Jess nodded. "The change been stressful, but the old ways were even more stressful."

Ron continued. "Sheila already knows this, but I want to make clear to everyone that the Ladder framework will make this Customer Experience process – and others – scaleable. For example, pretty soon, each time we add a new store, we'll have a process baked into the system for the new managers to follow."

"This means that Sheila won't have to be at each new store transferring her knowledge and expertise. It also means that if Sheila should leave the company, her expert knowledge will be available to future teams. This is what we mean by building a knowledge base – Level 4 on the Ladder."

"All this is going to leave me some free time," said Sheila. "Maybe I can

add to that knowledge base – figure out new and better ways of bringing in more customers."

*   *   *   *   *

Natural Bounty is now in the process of attaining Level 3 on the Ladder. It can be said to have reached this level when the majority of its core processes are rated either green or yellow. Please take a look at the Process Health Measurement chart below.

In this section, we'll take a brief look at Level 3 and the upper levels of the Ladder. Reaching each of these levels incorporates a specific kind of intelligence into an organization. An intelligent enterprise needs all of these skills to function in today's world.

Process Health Measurement Criteria

Process Health Measurement	Details
RED	•Process is ineffective and/or inefficient •Outputs do not meet customer requirements •Metrics are not identified or tracked •Performance problems exist, no cross-functional alignment
YELLOW	•Process output meets basic customer requirements •Metrics are identified, but require significant improvement •Some operational problems need resolution •Better cross-functional alignment and interlock required
GREEN	•Process meets customer needs in an efficient manner •Metrics show positive improvement trends •Process is well documented and actively managed •Effective cross-functional alignment and interlock

Level 3: Information

Reaching Level 3 is a milestone because this is the point at which most important processes are able to utilize information. The relevant information that is needed to run the process smoothly and seamlessly is delivered automatically into the information systems. And this, in turn, enhances communication, collaboration, effective decisions and overall performance.

This is information that enables more effective business decisions. The ability to obtain key information on a regular basis is the first quality of an intelligent organization. The better the information, the more intelligent are the business decisions.

Level 3 is also a plateau from which to ascend to the higher levels of the Ladder. For example, once electronic information is available, it is now possible to make it retrievable and reusable for future users. This is approaching Level 4 on the Ladder

Level	Example
Facts	Multiple customer databases – no organization
Data	Integrated database - ERP
Information	Information View - OLAP
Knowledge	Knowledge base - FAQ
Understanding	Share Knowledge across roles – Proactive Actions
Enabled Intuition	Insightful Business Decisions – Breakthrough Visionary Results

Level 4: Knowledge

At Level 4 of the Ladder, knowledge is no longer an individual asset. Everyone who solves a business problem feeds that solution into an electronic "library," or knowledge base, of repeatable solutions. This means that when this problem – or a similar problem – occurs again, those people dealing with it will have help in determining the best course of action simply by referring to the knowledge base. *At Level 4, knowledge and experience are retrievable and reusable.*

At Natural Bounty, for example, this means that the process of bringing practices and products in new stores into alignment with existing stores will be repeatable. And if Sheila – the expert in this process – should leave the company, this will not be a disaster because her knowledge will be stored in her unit's library of repeatable solutions. In addition, any experience that Sheila and her team gains – any lessons learned – will be added to this knowledge base.

This is one example of how the Ladder can bring an expert's knowledge to an average employee. By employing this "stored experiential information" this employee is now able to achieve the same results as the expert. In other words, he or she is able to perform more *intelligently.*

This why building knowledge databases for each business domain is one way that a business grows in intelligence. Key information can now be gleaned not just from present-time sources, but from sources that organize past experience.

Level 5: Understanding

Once there are knowledge bases, an organization has what it needs to go on to Level 5. "Understanding" can best be described as a personal "internalization" of a set of knowledge achieved through close contacts and long experience with a specific business domain. This understanding can be assisted by adding new tools to the information system; these tools can present business trends and even recommend courses of action.

Imagine that everyone in your organization understands not only its vision and goals, but also the role that each of them plays in achieving these goals. Imagine further that the understanding enables robust collaboration among all groups working on business processes.

When there is clear understanding among all players of the company's direction and key challenges, cross-functional collaboration and brainstorming sessions can reach new levels. In addition, meetings are shorter, more creative and more fun. The discussion is enriched instead of divided by all the different perspectives from the various business roles. And all this raises the quality of decision making.

This is life at Level 5. Is it achievable? Absolutely. The kind of star companies portrayed in Chapter 2 have attained Level 5. At Southwest Airlines, FedEx, and other world class companies, employees at all levels understand what their company is about, as well as their roles in contributing to its success.

This is also the level that Natural Bounty is trying to achieve by retaining its best employees. The company wants experienced, knowledgeable managers and front line employees. They want people who understand what Natural Bounty is trying to achieve and can collaborate at a high level of understanding.

At Level 5, collaboration takes on a new dimension. A business can now perform "what-if" analyses on very complex problems because the journey from Levels 1 through 4 has given people a common framework and language to work with. This standardization of knowledge concept allows a "what-if" brainstorming session to occur more rapidly and produce more meaningful results.

This give and take is among people who understand the goals of the company, but have different areas of expertise. High-level collaboration of this kind can be especially powerful because a kind of synergy is created where the whole is greater than the sum of the parts. The collaborative effort is now aimed at improving processes and company performance, not just making processes run more smoothly. Innovation of all kinds is encouraged and enabled.

Level 6 Enabled intuition

We have now reached the rarefied atmosphere at the top level of the Ladder. This is the level of out-of-the-box solutions and the "aha!" moments. Enabled intuition can be described as knowing or sensing without rational process. As Zen-like as this sounds, enabled intuition is an extremely powerful state from which to operate. The business intelligence attained via Levels 1 through 5 improves the probability of a visionary breakthrough at Level 6.

Enabled intuition is the creative mind at work. Creativity, however, does not emerge from a vacuum. Artists, for example, must practice long hours at the mechanics of their chosen endeavor before they are able to produce works of value. Any inventor will tell you of the necessity of total immersion in a technology before any improvements to that technology occur to him or her.

Similarly, our observation is that useful business intuition cannot occur without a deep understanding of the business domain. People who have attained Level 5 Understanding are much more likely to know intuitively what course of action will benefit the business in any situation. It is also from this profound understanding that individuals perceive unusual relationships and draw new conclusions. If a company can get a small subset of their employees at this level, they will have a higher probability of creating visionary breakthroughs.

Most innovations combine existing technologies and knowledge bases. For example, Apple's iPOD integrates the existing knowledge bases of music downloading, PDA device concepts and automated web pay technology in a new way. The only new idea here is the integration of these knowledge bases into an innovative – and extremely profitable – product.

Smart managers will encourage this Level 6 thinking at all levels of the organization. A shipping clerk who suggests a change in the shipping process could save a business millions simply because he or she was encouraged and rewarded for thinking out of the box. To encourage this type of thinking, a company can define and install a suggestion box program with rewards sponsored by the top executives.

Building the Intelligent Organization

Meeting the challenges of today's market place means employing all available resources in a business in a way that brings them ever closer to their objectives. These resources include all the different kinds of intelligence that the Ladder helps to develop.

Intelligence is a growing thing. A truly intelligent person is always aware that he or she still has much to learn – and the same is true of a business. The great companies – the IBMs, the GEs, the HPs – are continually trying new business models and bringing new products and services to market. They are never complacent. They work smart.

This chapter has described the ways in which an organization can grow continually smarter. These involve the optimal employment of all available resources, from human intelligence to machine intelligence, from understanding to enabled intuition.

In the challenging business environment of the 21st century, an enterprise needs as much intelligence as it can muster. In the next chapter we'll discuss this environment – and the ways in which the Ladder framework can help a business meet these challenges and thrive well into the future

.

Tom's Takeaways
A New Kind of Alignment

Until the latter half of the 20th century, almost all organizations functioned as hierarchies: the military, families, churches, governments and businesses. Historically speaking, command and control from the top helped to sustain many of the old values, like respect for authority, discipline and order. For businesses, they also promoted alignment, focus and clear accountability.

The recent evolution of business models parallels the evolution of society. During the latter half of the 20th century, the concept of unquestioned obedience to authority was increasingly challenged in many arenas. In response, a number of organizations began to reorganize around more democratic, collaborative models. In the business world, a new, educated workforce, particularly in the field of information technology, made it clear that they preferred a more open, freewheeling atmosphere. Managers noticed that open workplaces encouraged values like creativity and responsibility – which, in turn, led to enhanced performance.

The challenge for managers is how to reap the benefits of a loose authority structure, while still retaining alignment and focus. How do you ensure that a group of independently minded employees will accomplish organizational goals in a coordinated manner?

The integrating factor in the hierarchical organization is the unquestioned authority of superiors in a pyramid-shaped command structure. The Ladder seeks to replace this rigid structure with a framework constructed around common purposes.

In the Ladder model, alignment of purpose is built into the planning process, allowing authority to be spread out at all levels. In contrast to a hierarchical organization, a collaborative community organized around common purposes can retain an open atmosphere, while supporting a new kind of alignment and focus.

8 The Corporation in the 21st Century

Aspiration or Desperation?

In previous chapters, we've discussed the advantages of adopting the Ladder framework. Companies may decide to evaluate and adopt the Ladder either from aspiration or desperation. Managers either perceive the need for greater intelligence to help them move ahead, or they realize that their business is going to fail without it.

Forward-looking firms are aware that today's business climate demands constant growth and innovation. On the other hand, firms that hold fast to their current business model, however successful, often find their market share slowly being eaten away by more agile, innovative competitors.

In this chapter, we're going to look at some of the challenges of doing business in the 21st century. These include fast-moving competitors, customers who expect high quality and low prices, and unforgiving investors. Compliance with government regulations has recently become a key challenge as a result of the Sarbanes-Oxley – and other – legislation.

It can be instructive to examine those forces that have brought about this dynamic, fast moving, consumer-based world. In this next section, we'll do our best to condense the last thirty years into about two pages. Then we'll join the CEET team at Natural Bounty to view how they are coping with some of the demands of growth. Finally, in Section 3, we'll suggest ways that the Ladder framework can help businesses prosper in this high-pressure, demanding environment.

In a time not so long ago...

In the not-too-distant past, business moved at a much slower pace. In those days, the most important information about a company could be captured by perusing its balance sheets and quarterly financial statements. Strange as it may seem today, it was actually possible for most firms to predict revenues for the next year by looking at performance in the previous year.

In the sleepy financial industry, people joked about the bankers' 3-4-4 Rule: "Pay 3% on savings, lend the money out at 4% and be on the golf course by 4 PM."

Starting around 1975, however, a new political and economic environment began to emerge. Arguing that American business was being stifled by government regulations, many in government and the private sector advocated a "self-regulating marketplace."

One of the first manifestations of this new marketplace was the relaxation of regulations governing monopolistic industries. As communications giants, airlines, utilities, brokerages and others were deregulated, a host of smaller service providers and manufacturing firms grew to fill the void. These new firms used technological innovations and new business models to become competitive. Think of Apple ambushing IBM or a multitude of firms with new copy machines almost overwhelming Xerox. Count the hundreds of new telephone companies (include the cell phone providers). Think of thousands of new companies doing business over the Internet while taking market share away from traditional businesses.

During the 1980s and '90s, this deregulation was extended to international trade. Assisted by global political changes, barriers to the free flow of goods and services began to fall all over the world, encouraging the spread of new and existing businesses. Many enterprises with limited markets in their own countries discovered multitudes of customers overseas. Corporations lowered their costs by buying on the international markets and by expanding into cheaper labor markets. Today, the rule is that work will eventually be done where it is done best. "Best" is measured in terms of labor price and productivity.

This expansion into global markets advanced as contractual agreements were standardized in a growing number of countries. Strategic alliances and extended value chains, following their domestic growth, now regularly cross national boundaries.

At the same time, entrepreneurs with innovative concepts soon discovered that they had friends in a growing venture capital industry. Encouraged by the success of many startups, venture specialists were able to corral large amounts of capital from eager investors and channel it into start-up companies. This has continued, in spite of economic ups and downs. Venture capital firms raised and invested just

$600 million in 1980 and $4 billion in 1987. By 2006, this figure had risen to $6.3 billion in the second quarter alone.

The judicious use of stock options in lieu of high salaries allowed these new firms to hire top people willing to bet that their abilities could raise the value of the company's stock. Suppliers, too, were often persuaded to take payment in the form of options. The availability of capital combined with the clever use of options has enabled multitudes of start-ups to compete successfully with large established companies.

And, of course, throughout this period, a revolution in information technology was taking place (as discussed in Chapter 6). Vast new industries came into being, spawning multiple new enterprises and challenging old methods of operating. This revolution, of course, continues today.

A Synergy of Forces

All these forces have played critical roles in creating a new business landscape, but the overall geography of this landscape has been formed by these forces acting in concert. The new economy has come about not just because the personal computer was invented, but also because of the innovative use of venture capital and stock options, not just as a result of the breakup of AT&T and other monopolies, but also because barriers to free trade have come down. It is the synergy of these forces acting together that has effected this transformation in the space of a few decades.

The end result of this synergy is an environment so friendly to commerce that ever-growing numbers of entrepreneurs are encouraged to enter the marketplace. This explosion of new enterprises has created unrelenting competition, both domestically and globally.

It has also created intense pressure from customers, who have come to expect quality products and personalized service at low prices. Because of the number of alternatives available – and the ease of finding them on the Internet – both business and consumer customers have become harder to please.

Investors too are presented with a multitude of opportunities all over the world. If shareholders fail to perceive a continuous growth in value, they are likely to move their money very rapidly to another, more promising, venue.

This is the brave new world of the 21st century – a world of great opportunities for entrepreneurs, but also one of intense challenges. In this world, the survivors will be the companies that are able to create great new products and bring them to market rapidly. These are the firms that stay ahead of the markets, please their investors by constantly growing in value and bore the regulators by always staying in compliance.

The purpose of this book, of course, is to help your company become one of these firms. A business that excels in employing information keeps an alignment of purpose and stimulates innovation, is a business that sees opportunities instead of difficulties in today's marketplace. To this firm, globalization means a larger customer base, new technologies present new opportunities and competitors are seen as stimulators to even greater achievement. This is the kind of enterprise that the Ladder can create.

The rest of this chapter describes the ways in which the Ladder can help companies deal with the challenges of the 21st century. Let's start by taking a look at how Natural Bounty is dealing with its new role as a public company.

Natural Bounty: New Challenges

Natural Bounty was founded in 1975, just as the pace of economic activity was beginning to take off. From a single natural foods market, the company gradually acquired and built sixty more stores over a thirty-year period. In 2004, encouraged by the growing popularity of natural and organic products, management decided to bring the firm public. The Initial Public Offering in 2005 went well and, over the next few months, the price of the stock doubled.

Flush with cash from the stock sale, management began a buying spree over the next two years, picking up a total of fifty new stores – both individual organic markets and small chains. Suddenly, Natural Bounty was an up-and-coming public company with new opportunities – and plenty of growing pains.

When we joined our friends in the Corporate Effectiveness and Efficiency Team in Chapter 3, they were just beginning to understand what resources they needed to cope with their new growth. Since that time, they have also begun to comprehend the challenges of becoming a public company. We join them now as they discuss these new challenges.

* * * * *

Jess was speaking to Emily and Sheila as Ron and Jeffrey came in the door.

"Now that we're a public company, there are suddenly a lot of people who are very interested in what we do: investors, analysts, government people – the SEC, Sarbanes-Oxley auditors...."

Emily interrupted. "Jess, could you explain once and for all why Sarbanes-Oxley is such a big deal. I know it's about keeping people accountable, but why is this so difficult?"

Jess nodded. "Sarbanes-Oxley is an attempt to restore public trust after the Enron debacle and other high profile disasters. The SOX requirements are about accountability – CEOs, Boards of Directors and other executives are not only accountable for their own decisions, but also for the actions of anybody else in the company."

"For instance," added Ron, "the top guys at Enron said, 'We didn't know what was going on. All this wrongdoing was done by people at lower levels.' Sarbanes-Oxley says, 'Well, if you're in upper management, you have to know what's going on in your company at every level.' This means that you have to have mechanisms in place to that will monitor key transactions and flag you when any processes or transactions get out of whack. Every public firm has to have these internal control structures – and they have to demonstrate that they're effective."

"This sounds like a positive thing," said Emily. "So why is everybody complaining?"

"Some people are complaining," answered Ron, "because they feel that compliance has become too onerous – that the government's gone too far and needs to find a new balance. But most are complaining because their companies are not set up to comply. Tracking processes and decisions are a major problem for most companies.

"For example, you've got to have accountability – you need to know who approved what and when. This requires a workflow approval trail that's automated. 'Here's the purchase requisition, now you've got a purchase order, now the writing of the checks....' You've got to have these audit trails automated – and there are hundreds and hundreds of them."

"Ah," said Emily, "I'm beginning to see where this is leading us."

Jeffrey put his palms together and gave Emily a little bow. "*All* roads lead to the Ladder," he intoned.

Sheila smiled. "That's it, Jeff. Now you're getting it. Seriously, the Ladder provides the kind of visibility and tracking that SOX demands. But this is a good thing. People should be happy about SOX. These are all things that they need to know anyway. If I can find the owner of a process or track a workflow with a few clicks, I'm that much further ahead."

"Well put," said Ron. "I also want to point out that Sarbanes-Oxley isn't the only government regulation we deal with. There's the SEC reporting, there are state regulations – and everything's different in Canada. One of the first things Randall did when I became CIO was to put me in charge of overall compliance. At that time, it was a nightmare – we had so many different systems and spreadsheets. But this is changing as we get our new systems up and running. Anything I need to know about the state of compliance with each set of regulations will be right there on my display device."

"And, according to Sheila, these are things that you – and we – need to know anyway," said Emily.

"Absolutely," said Ron.

"Let me give you an example from Finance, Em," said Jess." We had this accountant in one of our new stores who was overly enthusiastic about how much money the store was making. Put simply, he just wasn't deducting certain expenses on the balance sheet. Now, over-reporting earnings can get you in trouble with the SOX people. That's what they did big time at Worldcom and a few other places. But if this guy is not getting it right, that's something we need to know right away, regardless of SOX or any other agency."

"So it's not just wrongdoing," said Emily. "We also need to catch honest mistakes and different ways of reporting."

"We need to see it all," answered Jess. "What appears to us as an honest mistake may look very different to a SOX investigator. Remember, another one of the frauds at Worldcom was underreporting expenses. When it all blew up, the auditors figured that the underreporting of expenses and the addition of bogus revenues added up to about $11 billion. This was just before the company declared bankruptcy."

Emily whistled. "Okay," she said, "I'm beginning to see why getting the reporting right is so important. Everything needs to be visible."

Jess nodded. "As a finance person, this is one of the things that attracted me to the Ladder. In Finance, everything's visible. We can aggregate all the income in any way we want, right up the total gross for the year. Then we can de-aggregate these figures down to income for each market. We can find the income for any given month or week for a market in Calgary or Salt Lake City. We have visibility – and we have the kind of answers we need to take action."

"I see the Ladder helping provide this is the kind of visibility to everyone in the company. People will get their questions answered. That's what the BRIA is all about. For example, in HR, you'll get your questions answered about desirable versus non-desirable exits – and this will allow you to take whatever action you need. Top management gets any information it needs. It's like a company-wide accounting system – everything's transparent and traceable."

Emily nodded. "Accounting…accountability. So, public or private, we need this visibility."

"We sure do," answered Jess. In the past, we sort of just got by, like a lot of companies. Going public ups the ante. Now you have to be able to track all the things that you should have been tracking anyway. If you don't, you can get in big trouble."

"With the Feds, you mean," said Jeffrey.

"Not just the Feds," answered Jess, "but the whole investment world – the analysts, the investors. If we slip up – make a poor earnings projection or have to re-state our financials – suddenly, we're written up in the financial papers. 'Natural Bounty seems to be floundering....' Then the stock starts to slide. It's a whole new world being a public company."

"We need to have answers for investors too," said Sheila. "One of them called up Investor Relations the other day and asked if all the produce we buy in Latin America is purchased according to fair trade guidelines. You know, giving the farmers a fair income. We don't know the answer to that, but we should. If it turns out we're dealing with middlemen who are exploiting the farmers, we're in for a bad time with our socially responsible investors and our customers."

Jeffrey leaned forward. "But, just like the information for SOX, this is something we need to know anyway. We don't want to be exploiting farmers."

"Visibility," said Ron. "It's all about visibility."

* * * * *

Challenges and Solutions in the 21st Century

In the first part of the chapter, we reviewed the forces that have created the supercharged economic world of the 21st century. In this section, we'll explore the demands that this environment places on individual businesses. And we'll demonstrate how the Ladder can help you transform these demands into opportunities.

Compliance

At Natural Bounty, the CEET team is dealing with the challenge of complying with a number of different government regulations. Because the company has stores in a number of different states as well as Canadian provinces, this is a critical issue for them. In addition, as a public company issuing securities, there are numerous regulatory agencies that are very interested in seeing that securities laws are observed.

Natural Bounty has been trying to comply with all these requirements with its fragmented, unintegrated information systems, processes and control points. This unintegrated system may be all too familiar to many managers. Trying to find information about company-wide practices in a consistent and cohesive way with systems designed for various silos can be daunting, to say the least. Searching manually through spreadsheets for key pieces of data can be frustrating and time-consuming, to say nothing of error-prone. At Natural Bounty, this fragmentation meant that they failed audits again and again. This cost the company large amounts of money in penalty fees. In addition, it also had to expend a great deal of effort trying to satisfy the auditors.

Sarbanes-Oxley requires, among other things, that companies establish compliance standards and procedures to be followed by all employees. They must further demonstrate that they are able to monitor and track transactions, as well as raise red flags when any activity is not in compliance.

This is accomplished by mapping all the core business processes that will be monitored and governed. Then, by following the Business Role Intelligence Analysis (BRIA) procedure, those in charge of compliance can formulate the questions they need answered. This input then feeds into the architecture and design of the information technology (IT) systems.

In the final step, IT experts will choose a system to provide managers with the information and visibility they need to comply with each set of regulations. Then, after the new system goes live, the owner of each business process is clearly identified and audit trails are automated and easy to retrieve. *The "who, what, where and when" of business processes and projects in progress are now easily monitored.*

As Ron and Jess advised the CEET team, this transparency, visibility and access to key information is critical for the company, not just for the auditors. In his recent book, *The Joy of SOX*, Hugh Taylor emphasizes this very point. Taylor argues that, regardless of Sarbanes-Oxley, a firm has to have accurate information about anything that affects its financial statements. He holds that the best way to capture this information is by automating business activities and internal operations. We couldn't agree more.

To Taylor, SOX presents an opportunity for a company to gain greater visibility into its own operations. Because the Ladder framework brings about this visibility, this is an example of how the Ladder transforms a potential problem into an opportunity.

Competition

What do businesses need to cope with the relentless competition in today's markets? A realistic and inspiring vision must come first, but once a business has decided on its vision, the focus shifts to the best ways of translating this vision into reality. A whole list of capabilities may come to mind, but we can narrow this down to just three critical areas: increased intelligence, networking capability and innovation.

1. **Intelligence**. In the Ladder framework, the alignment of vision, strategies, processes and information is what creates intelligence and robust collaboration. The intelligent business functions at Level 3 and up. Businesses operating at these higher levels of information and intelligence have a distinct competitive advantage over businesses that are still functioning at Levels 1 and 2.

   In the intelligent business, the right information is delivered to the right people at the right time. The goal is an organization where effective business decisions are based on quality information and vigorous collaboration. These decisions, in turn, enable a business to be proactive in its ability to envision new markets, new products and future economic environments.

   Effective decisions then lead to the seamless translation of a vision into an actual product or service. In this case, "seamless" implies a shorter time to market with less expense, as well as higher quality products with greater profit margins. This is the intelligent business at work.

2. **Networking**. The networking capacity of an organization is measured by its ability to create and communicate critical information within the business and create a community of collaborators. Most enterprises today include disparate business units, complex supply chains, and far-flung strategic

partners. A business that has mastered its networking capabilities will be able to communicate and collaborate across departmental, organizational and geographical boundaries to coordinate the movement and transactions of goods, services and information throughout the extended enterprise.

As an example, Natural Bounty now has 110 markets spread over the United States and Canada. One of the processes that Sheila is involved in, as Director of Purchasing, is the optimization of purchasing procedures. Certain questions arise, such as: "When is it cost effective for all stores to order certain products in bulk and when is it better for individual stores to order locally?" This optimization may include factors other than just cost. For instance, in most areas, customers have made it clear that they want locally-grown produce whenever possible.

This desire for local produce, however, has led to instances where buyers for several Natural Bounty stores in nearby towns have competed with each other for produce from local farmers. Sheila would like to replace this competition with a networking system that would enable cooperative purchasing among possible competitors. In fact, she would like to optimize and rationalize the entire purchasing system.

To accomplish this task, her team followed the Ladder framework. They first considered the vision and mission of Natural Bounty, the core objectives of the company and promises made to their partners and customers. They then defined the core processes that needed to be automated to support that vision. They asked the process owners what key questions they needed the system to answer (in the BRIA process). Once the system is fully up and running, it will provide key information to all players in a given process, enabling them to network productively.

Many companies have the added challenges of language and cultural differences in communicating with their suppliers and strategic partners. Achieving collaborative networking among all these diverse businesses requires a sharing of first class information. A manager in New York needs to be looking at the same key information on her computer screen as her counterpart in Calcutta.

3. **Innovation**. Since our next chapter is largely about the importance of innovation, we will simply state here that a business' ability to keep improving and enhancing products and services, fulfill new demands and create new markets are critical skills in today's markets. Customers want products that not only meet their needs but anticipate them. Investors want their company to be in the forefront of their field.

All this requires that a business have the skills to stay in tune with its customers' desires as well as search out possible new customer bases. Once a new product has been decided upon, bringing it to market in record time has also become a necessary skill. In Chapter 9, we will examine just how the Ladder can provide these skills that facilitate the process of innovation.

Retrospective | In this chapter, we started with a brief retrospective on the creation of the modern business world. We then looked in on a meeting of managers who are attempting to deal with the demands of this world. And, finally, we identified a few more of these demands and suggested ways in which the Ladder framework can help. The exacting environment of the 21st century requires that a business employ its resources in the most effective ways. A business operating at the higher levels of the Ladder is able to maximize all its resources. The challenges that discourage other firms are treated as opportunities by the intelligent enterprise.

Smart businesses are aware that constant innovation is the key to survival and success in today's world. In the next chapter, we'll examine how an intelligent business goes about the process of innovation, from concept to creation.

Tom's Takeaways
Level 3 in the Medical World

The scenarios described in this book have been primarily those of the business world. The Ladder framework, however, can work equally well for all kinds of non-business organizations. Serving customers in an effective and efficient manner is the aim of most institutions, whether or not they earn profits. This means that employing information in an intelligent manner should be a goal of any forward-looking organization.

Unfortunately, until recently, most Health Maintenance Organizations (HMOs) have operated at Levels 1 and 2, with poorly organized facts and data. Medical models for the treatment of many diseases have often been based on inadequate research or even guesswork. One doctor, David Eddy, M.D., has made it his personal crusade to find the best treatments based on hard evidence.

Eddy has developed a computer model called "Archimedes" that simulates the actual biology of the human body. Using this model, Eddy was able to develop a greatly improved protocol for treatment of diabetes. Kaiser Permanente, one of the largest HMOs, has adopted this protocol with excellent results. Patient care has been improved and costs have been lowered.

Archimedes takes masses of data and uses it to answer questions like, "What are the most effective and least costly treatments for diabetes?" Sound familiar? By answering key questions and producing useful Information that can be stored and referenced, Archimedes and Dr. Eddy are operating at Levels 3 and 4. Dr. Eddy has been applying his "evidence-based medicine" to other diseases and the medical world is listening.

Chapter

9 Innovation and Excellence

Creativity plus implementation equals innovation.
Jim Collins

Around 1990, 3M researchers were presented with a challenge. Most screens for portable computers were 8.4-inch black and white displays. But users were telling manufacturers that they wanted larger screens with color. Because color displays use more power, the computer makers were looking for batteries with more power and longer lives.

Some engineers at 3M Corp saw the problem differently. What if, instead of adding battery power, more light could be directed at the user's eyes? 3M was already producing transparent films for other applications; what if they could produce a "light-enhancement" film?

This was the genesis of one of the company's most popular products. Today, virtually every flat screen display, portable or desktop, employs a 3M-designed ultrathin plastic film. The film enhances the brightness and the clarity of the image. This is especially useful in portables because it obviates the need for more bulky and expensive batteries.

This is a prime example of what is meant by an "out-of-the-box solution." Jay Ihlenfeld, senior vice-president for research and development at 3M, explains it this way: "So, when a customer says, 'We need a battery with a longer life or one that can put out more energy,' 3M knows to ask the next question: 'Why do you need that?' It's our job to drill down to understand what is the underlying solution."

What makes a company innovative? Why is 3M near the top of the list of innovative firms? What places diverse firms like Apple, GE, Google and Virgin Atlantic in this select group? These are some of the questions we plan to answer in this chapter. Other questions relate to the Ladder of Business Intelligence. "In a survey[3] conducted by the Boston Consulting Group, the following ten companies were rated the highest in Innovation in 2006: Apple, Google, 3M, Toyota, Microsoft, General Electric, Procter & Gamble, Nokia, Starbucks, and IBM. The question is what made those 10 companies rate higher then others. Does the Ladder encourage and enable innovation? In what ways?

The Innovation Economy

In case you haven't noticed, innovation is in. *Business Week*[4] devoted much of its August 1, 2005 issue to the subject. In the editors' words:

---

3. The complete survey can be found on the following URL: http://www.bcg.com/publications/files/2006_Innovation_Survey_report.pdf
4. Business Week, August 1, 2005, Special Edition: complete story at http://www.businessweek.com/magazine/content/05_31/b3945401.htm

"The new core competence is innovation. The game is...about creativity, imagination and, above all, innovation."

In the previously referenced Boston Consulting Group survey, these executives emphasized that innovation has become an essential element for success in their various industries. However, more than half of these business leaders said they were disappointed in their return on investment in innovation.

What's going on here? There is general agreement on the value of innovation, but many companies seem unable to generate good returns. What elements may be missing in these attempts at innovation? This is a question we will return to later in the chapter. Right now, let's look at a company that is successfully making the shift to a culture of innovation.

Here's a quote from Jeffey Immelt, GE's CEO: "We're measuring GE's top leaders on how imaginative they are. Imaginative leaders are the ones who have the courage to fund new ideas, lead teams to discover new ideas and lead people to take educated risks."

In 2003, Immelt introduced GE's Imagination Breakthrough projects. These projects currently consist of eighty initiatives with a total of $5 billion in funding. Immelt urged his managers to take risks, connect with customers and place big bets.

The IB projects are one of several that were designed to raise GE's organic growth from 5% to 8%, or 2-3 times that of world Gross Domestic Product (GDP). They have been successful in this goal during 2005 and 2006. In November of 2006, GE predicted double-digit growth for 2007.

In short, under Immelt's leadership since 2001, GE has shifted its emphasis from a process culture to an innovation culture.

We have chosen to focus on GE for good reason. Under Jack Welch, GE developed one of the best process cultures in the world. Efficiency, cost-cutting and continual improvement of operations were among the main factors that contributed to the company's success in the 1990s.

For Jeffrey Immelt to use that marvelous infrastructure as a base for his innovative ventures is a perfect logical progression. We have asserted throughout this book that the foundation for success is based on process optimization that is aligned with business strategy, people and information technology. Creating a culture of innovation is no exception. Imagination breakthroughs happen not just because somebody has a great idea, but because the infrastructure is in place to transform that idea into a great product or service.

The ten most innovative companies mentioned above are famous not just for great products, but for a rapid time to market. This kind of speed means that these companies have clearly designed and optimized the entire product life cycle. From idea, to concept, to prototype, to manufacturing, to marketing, to delivering products, to customer care, each step has been carefully thought out. These companies all operate at the higher levels of the Ladder.

This is the reason that we spent several chapters in this book outlining the ways in which an organization can improve its business processes. This is why we have emphasized the importance of quality information delivered to the right business role. Moving new products from concept to collect requires an infrastructure that operates at Levels 3 to 6.

Innovation at 3M

3M is the granddaddy of innovative cultures. Products introduced in the previous four years regularly make up about a third of their total sales; products introduced in the same year make up about a tenth of total sales. Here are the policies that have worked for 3M Corp for many decades:

1. **RD Spending**: 3M spends 6% to 7% of sales on R&D, about twice the spending of the average manufacturing company.

2. **Customer Contact**: Customers are encouraged to meet with company researchers to discuss their use of 3M products and to help generate new ideas.

3. **15 Percent Option**: A large number of employees can choose to spend up to 15% of their work week concentrating on individual projects of their own choice.

4. **Seed Capital**: Inventors first ask their managers for funding to develop their product ideas. If the managers refuse, the inventors have other in-house options to get the seed capital.

5. **Tolerance for Failure**: There is no punishment for failure of a venture. Participants retain their jobs. 3M has a history of turning initial failures into breakthrough products. For example, a weak adhesive product became the basis for the company's famous Post-it notes.

6. **Rewards for Success**: If a venture attains certain revenue levels, its team members receive promotions, raises and recognition.

7. **Profit Centers**: Business Units are split up when they reach a level of $200 to $300 million. Each business unit is run as a profit center. Most 3M employees participate in the company's profit-sharing plan.

(Summarized from the 3M Web site)

Innovating with the Ladder

Let's return, for a moment, to our question earlier in the chapter. What elements may be missing in the attempts at innovation in many firms?

For starters, in purely practical terms, if people spend 80% of their time on activities that can be logically simulated and executed by a machine, they're not going to have much time for creative thinking. This is a tremendous waste of human potential. This potential could be much better employed at improving, enhancing, achieving, developing and innovating. The Ladder sets up a framework that frees human intelligence to concentrate on innovation, be it improving a process or bringing a new product to market.

Secondly, in order to make the cycle time to market as short as possible, the infrastructure has to be in place to support the entire product life cycle. This means that processes like R&D, vendor relationship management, and pricing of all the products and services must already be in place. If this infrastructure is not in place, the ideas will die on the vine, no matter how inspired they are. It will simply take too long to bring a product to market if key opportunities are missed.

The Ladder framework enables organizations to streamline their operations – their people, processes and technologies – and optimize the level of automation. This creates an infrastructure able to bring ideas to the marketplace in a seamless manner.

What other qualities are inherent in the Ladder framework that encourage the skills and capabilities a business needs to become a master innovator?

First of all, the Ladder gets people involved in solving problems. Whether it's figuring out how to make a broken process work or deciding which questions you need answered to improve your performance, creative thinking is encouraged. This is the kind of creative thinking, for example, that 3M encourages in all its employees, not just its researchers.

Second, this creative thinking and planning results in processes that actually work. Consider GE and its remarkable process culture: this is what has enabled them to accomplish great feats of innovation. Their infrastructure supports all stages of the innovation process.

Third, by creating an infrastructure that provides key information to each business role, the performance of each process is leveraged. Attaining Level 3 enables business intelligence to be generated, stored, retrieved and managed in a manner that supports a business in its mission, objectives and strategies.

Level 3 also affects the kind of collaboration that is vital to the innovative process. Bringing a new product to market involves collaboration among multiple business units, vendors, suppliers and partners. It involves the ability to communicate across functional lines and geographical distances. This kind of collaboration is a critical factor in the success of any business. Smooth and effective collaboration among all players results in high quality products brought to market in a speedy manner.

Any company that brings out numerous new products needs a knowledge base of best practices. This may also include market best practices that can be leveraged through external sources. An innovator needs immediate answers to questions like: "How was that similar product brought to market three years ago?" The prime mover of that earlier product may have left the company, but, at Level 4, his or her knowledge is stored, updated and easily retrieved in the company intellectual property.

3M Corp supports "Technology Forums," both formal and informal. These forums may involve formal meetings among scientists from different laboratories in the company. Informal sharing is also encouraged via email; there is a comprehensive email directory that supports this. The company makes awards for successful sharing of new technology between business units. This is Level 5 intelligence at work.

When a company is operating successfully at Level 5, there is an understanding of the overall goals and objectives of the enterprise. This understanding forms a common ground from which creative people from different areas of expertise can collaborate fruitfully.

Finally, 3M provides us with a fine example of life at Level 6 with the company's "15% Option." Allowing creative individuals to spend 15% of their workweek pursuing individual projects of their own choice is a powerful example of the kind of enabled intuition described in Level 6 of the Ladder. These projects need not be justified – or even disclosed – to a manager. 3M calls it giving people room to innovate.

The creative individuals at 3M are thoroughly grounded in the company's goals, customer needs and in their own area of expertise. Their projects may grow out of their own interests, but are the kind that will benefit the company. As we have indicated in our discussion of Level 6, this is the kind of grounding needed to go off into flights of practical fancy.

We will shift our focus now from innovation to a final look at the various ways that the Ladder can be employed. After that, we'll present some concluding thoughts.

Encouraging Innovation

When we speak of an innovative company, we're not talking about a business that is focused on the next big thing, but rather of a culture that continually stimulates innovation in large and small things. Here are some policies and practices that encourage innovation, distilled from a number of innovative cultures:

- A policy that integrates innovation into a company's culture
- A budget that is large enough to support superior R&D
- Formal incentives to take risks and think outside the box, coupled with a policy of tolerance for failure
- A process that enables a clear early stage review of projects, thus limiting risk exposure
- A collaborative organizational environment
- An infrastructure that enables a rapid time to market

The Ladder creates an infrastructure that encourages and enables all these innovative practices at every level of a business.

A Tool for Evaluation

In the fall of 2006, one of the authors attended a meeting of Venture Capitalists. The subject was the Ladder as an evaluation tool. For example, if a VC wants to look at the market for a product produced by Company C, he can evaluate the products and services of the company based on where they fit in the Ladder framework.

Say that Company C plans to deliver products that provide or enable knowledge at Level 4 or Level 5. Using the Ladder framework, the VC can now evaluate the maturity level at which Company C's target customers are presently employing information. If 90% of them are still at Levels 1 and 2, then they are not yet ready to purchase this high-level product. Company C's potential customers have now been reduced to only 10% of the target market – a figure that will severely impact its future earnings.

This diagnostic capability can also be of great value to a business. It can be employed as a framework to help managers evaluate their company in terms of its sophistication, process health and application of technology. It enables questions like, "Are we using information skillfully – or are we still at Levels 1 and 2?" This evaluation then enables them to decide on the next steps.

Once a business has performed an evaluation, the Ladder then becomes a set of guiding principles and a framework around which an enterprise can organize its operations. When an organization begins to adopt these principles, it can be said to be implementing the Ladder framework.

A number of highly successful companies have utilized the same methods we have advocated here. Companies like Southwest, FedEx, Apple and 3M have achieved great success, but they have achieved this through the process of trial and error. How much easier it would be to move ahead guided by a step-by-step process. Like the recipes of master chefs, our recipe for success enables normal people to achieve extraordinary results.

Looking Back | We described how to proceed in implementing the Ladder framework in Chapters 3 through 6. This involved employing human intelligence to improve business operations and determining what business intelligence was needed to leverage this process.

Then, in Chapter 7, we asked readers to take a look at the results of our journey. Did we successfully describe the process by which an intelligent organization can be created? Does this organization indeed have the capability to employ information skillfully, make effective decisions and attain a competitive advantage?

Chapter 8 placed an enterprise in the context of the 21st century. The increasingly demanding business environment of today requires that a business employ all its resources in an intelligent manner. It's no longer possible to waste resources and still compete successfully. The Ladder is about optimal employment of all resources.

Finally, in this chapter, we talked about the importance of innovation. If innovation is made up of creativity plus implementation of that creativity, then the Ladder provides both a foundation and a framework. It first ensures that a business has the capabilities to achieve a rapid cycle time to market. Then, at Level 5, the Ladder describes methods for creative collaboration at the level of understanding. A successful ascent through all the levels can lead to the enabled intuition of Level 6 – creative thinking grounded in a thorough knowledge of the company, its markets and the economic landscape.

The Intelligent Business

Let's take one more look at the qualities of an intelligent business.

The Intelligent Business:

- Employs human intelligence at its fullest capacity
- Employs business intelligence optimally
- Uses superior information to enable effective decision making, communication and robust cross functional collaboration
- Uses the above three capabilities to create seamless business processes and a robust infrastructure
- Encourages innovation at every level of the organization
- Employs all of the above capabilities to operate successfully in all business environments
- Is always proactive, never complacent.

The Intelligent Business imitates the elegant neural feedback loops of biological nervous systems. Its organizational nervous system smoothly connects a strategy to daily operations and decisions, just as the biological system coordinates the different organs and limbs of the body. When every individual and business unit is aware of the overall direction and strategy of the company, then each decision they make will be, by definition, intelligent and aligned. These decisions will also be swift.

Luckily, these abilities do not need to evolve over millennia, but can be acquired in a relatively short time. An upper-level organizational nervous system is a combination of human and machine intelligence acting in concert. The Ladder provides a framework for this happy collaboration.

Our goal in this book has been to describe the creation of an Intelligent Business. The way this is achieved is by ascending each step of the Ladder of Business Intelligence. This carefully arranged process will enable a business to attain its goals and fulfill its true potential. A business that functions at Levels 3 and up essentially plays in a different league than those companies still at Levels 1 and 2.

As each person in a company grows in skill and understanding, the combination of their efforts will lift the enterprise to new heights. There is a synergy here: collaboration among knowledgeable people creates an outcome greater than the sum of the parts. The result is a culture of innovation functioning at Levels 5 and 6 of the Ladder.

Information technology plays a key role in supporting this collaborative effort. With the right information delivered to the right people at the right time, core processes can be optimized and reconfigured when necessary. This is the Intelligent Business where People, Process and Technology work together to create a world-class enterprise. There is no good reason to be satisfied with anything less.

Glossary

Business Role Intelligence Analysis (BRIA) is a simple but powerful tool for assessing information technology needs. There are 12 steps to creating the BRIA matrix:

1. Identify core processes.
2. Identify key roles and decide which of these needs the BRIA.
3. Define the business role name.
4. Address the key business questions (1-10) that the business role needs answered in order to be successful.
5. Identify the information required to answer those questions.
6. Identify quality data sources needed in order to generate the information to answer those questions.
7. Evaluate the time/frequency. How often does the business role need the information in order to be successful?
8. Decide how the information will be presented.
9. Decide how the information will be displayed (PDA, e-mail, application, report).
10. Identify the core processes. What are the processes that will be an input or an output for this business role?
11. Determine any additional business roles involved.

12. Determine the current level on the Ladder of this business role and determine the desired level.

Once the BRIA has been completed for a specific set of roles within a business domain or business unit, it will become the baseline for a "Business Requirement Document." This specification precedes any assessment for a new information system.

Circle of Success is a ten step process that guides an organization through a successful implementation of LOBI and attain higher levels of intelligence throughout the organization.

Corporate Effectiveness and Efficiency Team (CEET) is an internal company team where the individuals on the team are chosen for the scope of their vision. These are people who understand where the company needs to go and what it will take to get it there. They are also chosen for their leadership abilities. They are visionaries who are also movers and shakers, individuals who can influence and inspire others to change.

Data is composed of organized facts. Imagine that the bulletin board has now been organized into categories: each note has been placed in a labeled section of the board. Searching for an item is now limited to searching within a particular category.

Enabled Intuition is a higher level of understanding that facilitates decision makers to intuitively choose the right course of action that will benefit the business in any situation. With enabled intuition decision making is refined to an art.

Facts represent the recording of an event or measure in the "real" world. Imagine a bulletin board with a number of post-it notes. Each of these notes contains certain facts, but they are totally unorganized. If you want to find an item in a particular category, you will have to search across the entire board.

Information is data that has been organized to answer a specific question. For example, there are now a number of Web sites where you can fill in the details about the kind of car you want. The site will then present you with a number of choices from sellers. Forget the post-it notes. Because your search has been automated, it has become much simpler and less time consuming. You now have the information you need to make a good decision on buying a car. Translated to a business environment, it means freedom from searching through scores of spreadsheets for bits of data. Instead, the information technology organizes facts and data according to the questions you need answered. A sales manager, for instance, might have the total sales for the last three months available on her display device. This enables her to view trends and take action accordingly.

Knowledge consists of information and the derived rules on how to use the information. It includes best practices and knowledge about trends and behavior.

Ladder of Business Intelligence (LOBI®) is a framework that consists of an intelligence model (6 levels of intelligence) and a process (circle of success) that, when followed in a logical sequence, can result in a company that uses business intelligence successfully.

Understanding is knowledge that is shared. It refers to the alignment that occurs throughout an organization when company visions, strategies, and rules are shared and understood at all levels.

A Tom's Takeaways : "What is Information?"

> I'm sure you all believe you know what information is, but after you complete this tutorial, I think you will have a different view. Good information allows you to make a valuable and high impact decision; But how do you know that you have good information vs. bad information vs. misinformation? Before we discuss information, let's define how information differs from data.
>
> *Information* is processed data from which a conclusion can be drawn and used to answer questions.
>
> *Data*, on the other hand, is a collection of raw facts which has to be put in context to become data.

Information differs from data in that it allows immediate decision making without further processing of data. Hence, information is created when human intelligence uses data within a specific context defined by the person seeking the information. In other words, when data is applied in the specific context in which it was created and further processed and interpreted by a decision maker to give it a 'meaning', it becomes information.

The usual purpose of information is to allow someone seeking to achieve certain goals to make appropriate and impacting decisions. For example, in the context of your corporation, which market segments are you doing well in and which market segments require additional focus, are some of the business questions that your management team is trying to address every day. They use market segment data, customer data, product data and sales data and apply complex logic (context) to come up with the information that is then used by your management to make informed investment decisions.

As a company it is your goal to create shareholder value and quality of information has direct impact on the quality of business decisions you make. Let's now look at how one can create good information.

Good information is created by implementing correct models that produce correct answers to insightful questions. The value of the resulting information is directly proportional to the business impact of the decision that has been enabled.

Therefore, we must all become very good at asking the right questions. If we ask the right questions, profits will follow. If we ask trivial questions, then the resulting information will have little impact on the business. For example, at the end of a quarter many companies try to optimize their manufacturing capacity to meet increased demand in a manner that optimizes revenue. Hence, they are gathering data about many operational fulfillment tasks that ship products to their customers. However, for the CEO and CFO, the real information is the answers to the following three questions: how many billings have we recorded (revenue), how many bookings have we made (orders) and how many orders are on the books for the next quarter (backlog). This information will have a high impact, since it will directly influence the earnings per share of the corporation as well as the forecasted earnings for the next quarter.

This view of information as an answer to a question is simple yet powerful. Some of these questions may be intuitive. Most of us spend our lives chasing facts and data, not information. For example, one can spend an entire day browsing data on the web and not be able to make one key decision due in part to not knowing the right questions to ask, as well as the web not being well organized to easily glean answers. On the other hand, if you do know the right question to ask, the search engine model attempts to get at what you are looking for through keyword-based filtering and intelligent ranking mechanisms.

The operational sequence is Question – Information – Decision (Q-I-D). This is the operational decision triangle of power. The mission of a Business Intelligence (BI) team is to partner with the other business units to create the correct information views for making fast and effective business decisions.

In summary, the right decision, by the right person at the right time is the oil for a smoothly running organization. Information provides correct answers to key questions. If the output from the computer does not answer a key question for you, then it is data and not information. Hence, it is the skill of creating the correct questions to achieve your goals that you should be focused on.

BI units should team with business units to enhance their information delivery capabilities as the business units define the critical business questions. You should support your BI team as they interact with you to better understand your information needs.

About the Authors

Jim Cates is currently the CIO of Altera, a Silicon Valley high-tech company with over a billion dollars in revenue. He has over 30 years of experience in the Information Technology field. He spent 20 years at IBM in various R&D management positions developing IT tools for thousands of customers. He has also spent 10 plus years In Silicon Valley as the CIO, VP/IT and Corporate Process Officer of four high-tech companies, each creating over $500 million in revenue.

Sam Gill is a professor in the Information Systems department at San Francisco State University. Dr. Gill's career spans five decades of computing from the infant days of MAMRAM, the Israeli Ministry of Defense Computing Center, through his latest professional engagements as a consultant to fortune 1000 companies and state and federal agencies. During this span, Dr. Gill has been involved in several IT start-ups as well as managed several computing centers. Dr. Gill's latest venture was DataWiz Centers, one of the first Microsoft Solution Provider partners and the first Microsoft certified training partner.

Dr. Gill publishes (articles, books, and courseware) and teaches in many areas of information systems focusing on strategy, management, and technology. Currently, he is collaborating with Dean Lane on a book: CIO Perspectives. Dr. Gill's current research interests include the strategic, tactical, and operational management of Information Systems (IS), Business Intelligence, Software Testing and Quality Assurance (SQA), Information Technology (IT) Budgeting, Offshore and Outsourcing of IT, Development methodologies and frameworks, and development architectures, platforms and languages including: .NET, PHP/MySQL, Ruby on Rails, Visual Basic, C#, AJAX, and Java. Dr. Gill holds a Ph.D. from the University of California, Berkeley.

Natalie Zeituny has over seventeen years of experience working with international, world-class corporations, specializing in business strategy, process management and systems technology design and implementation. Ms. Zeituny has held highly visible leadership positions with companies such as 3com, Palm, Brocade, and Comverse. She has designed & implemented corporate and IT process architecture, business effectiveness and efficiency models and aligned cross functional business operations.

In 2002 Ms. Zeituny founded and became the principal of NZconsulting, a Management Consulting firm which has served clients such as Palm, Seagate, Brocade, Network Appliance, Altera Yahoo, Safeway, and others. She is currently launching a new business using her past experience; she has architected a new integral system that enables a new business paradigm, language and practices to emerge. Conscious Business Center provides a framework for financial success through planned application of social consciousness, environmental sustainability, personal/ technological creativity and spiritual/human self- realization.

Create Thought Leadership for your Company

Books deliver instant credibility to the author. Having an MBA or PhD is great, however, putting the word "author" in front of your name is similar to using the letters PHD or MBA. You are no long Michael Green, you are "Author Michael Green."

Books give you a platform to stand on. They help you to:

- Demonstrate your thought leadership
- Generate leads

Books deliver increased revenue, particularly indirect revenue

- A typical consultant will make 3x in indirect revenue for every dollar they make on book sales

Books are better than a business card. They are:

- More powerful than white papers
- An item that makes it to the book shelf vs. the circular file
- The best tschocke you can give at a conference

Why wait to write your book?

Check out other companies that have built credibility by writing and publishing a book through Happy About

Contact Happy About at 408-257-3000 or go to http://happyabout.info.

Purchase at http://happyabout.info or at other
online and physical bookstores.

*Learn the tricks and
techniques you need to
be effective!*

This book outlines the
tools, methods, and
protocols of creating and
cultivating an online
network for global reach,
business and personal
support, and professional
success.

Paperback:$19.95 132pgs
eBook:$ 11.95 132pgs

*This book is for
managers and
decision-makers who
make things happen!*

Learn from an anthology
of contributing authors
and experts who share,
step-by-step, how to
justify and manage the
ROI for the Business
Rules Approach. The
book covers both the
business and

Paperback: $29.95 324pgs
eBook: $19.95 250pgs

Printed in the United States
150587LV00004B/28/A